Discovering Queens!

A Useful Guide to Queens, New York
by Steve Reichstein

28 PLACES TO LIVE

50 RECOMMENDED RESTAURANTS

50 PLACES TO PLAY

82 PHOTOGRAPHS

THE STEPHEN PRESS, INC.

For information, write:
The Stephen Press
P.O. Box 754111
Forest Hills, New York 11375

Library of Congress Cataloging-in-Publication Data:

Reichstein, Steve
Discovering Queens
1. Queens, New York-guide l. Title
2000   00-091845
ISBN 1-882608-24-0

Copyright   © 2000 by Steve Reichstein
First Edition, September 2000

Book Design by Marilyn Reichstein
Photos by Steve Reichstein, except pages 58, 65, 66, 75, 163 by Stephen Suckenik
Map ©AAA, Reproduced by permission

Published by The Stephen Press, Inc. in cooperation with H&M Productions II, Inc.
Printed in the United States of America.

Dedication

To my mother, Sarah Seidel Reichstein.
A courageous lady of generous spirit whose noble
aspirations and good works enriched my life and the lives
of many of those she touched.

28 QUEENS RESIDENTIAL AREAS

1. Addisleigh Park
2. Astoria
3. Auburndale
4. Bayside
5. Bowne Park
6. Briarwood
7. College Point
8. Douglaston
9. Flushing
10. Forest Hills Gardens
    & Vicinity
11. Forest Hills—
    North of Queens Blvd.
12. Forest Hills—
    The Closes
13. Hollis
14. Holliswood
15. Jackson Heights
16. Jamaica
17. Jamaica Estates
18. Kew Gardens
19. Kew Gardens—
    Park Lane South
20. Laurelton
21. Long Island City
22. Malba
23. Richmond Hill—
    Condo
24. Richmond Hill North
25. Ridgewood—
    Sixty-Ninth Avenue
26. Ridgewood—
    Stockholm Street
27. St. John's University—
    82nd Road
28. Sunnyside

O=Highway Interchange

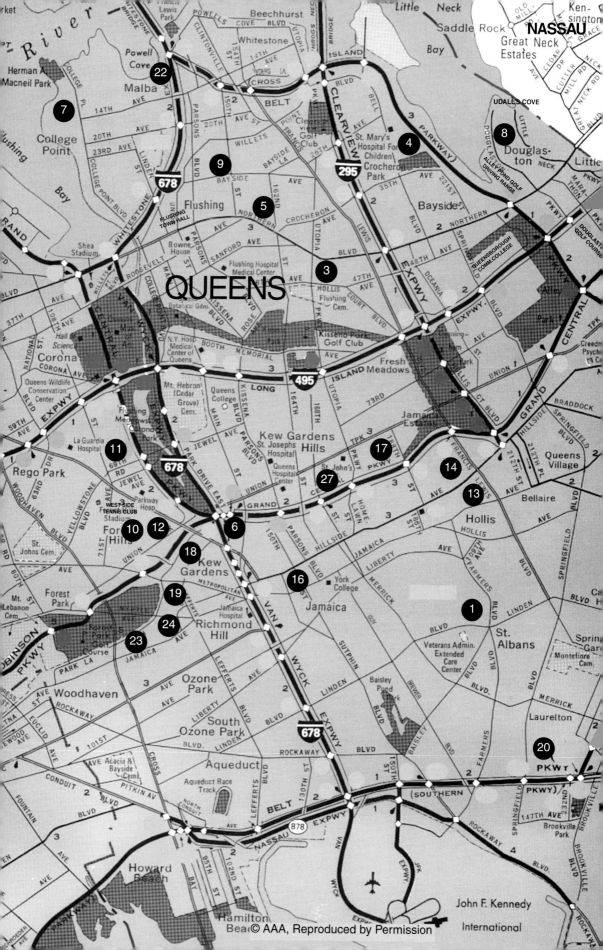

About the Author

Born and raised in Brooklyn, Steve Reichstein is a product of the New York City Public Schools and Hunter College. He received a Master of City Planning degree from the University of Pennsylvania. Steve moved to Queens twenty years ago when he returned to New York City with his wife and two daughters after an eight-year sojourn in Pittsburgh where he was the Deputy Director of Comprehensive Planning and Director of Community Development for the City of Pittsburgh.

Looking for affordable housing with good public schools, Steve settled in Forest Hills where he still resides. He has worked in New York City for the City Planning Department, Office of Management and Budget, and in Community Development. He recently retired as an Assistant to the President of the Borough of Brooklyn.

Steve was born in Brooklyn, went to college in the Bronx, and lived and worked in Manhattan. He loves New York City for its diversity, wide range of cultural experiences, opportunities, and good restaurants. He loves gardening and is a certified "City Tree Pruner." This is his first published book; he is working on a memoir of his one-year trip around the world.

Acknowledgments

The numerous field trips and days spent reading and researching the material for this book would all have been for naught had it not been for the help of friends, family, and colleagues, as well as those who have previously written books and material on subjects covered in this book.

Six books have been especially helpful: *Community District Needs Queens*, the City of New York Department of City Planning; *Historic Preservation In Queens*, Jeffrey A. Kroessler and Nina S. Rappaport; *AIA Guide to New York City*, Elliot Willensky and Norval White; *If You're Thinking of Living In...*, the New York Times Company; *Old Queens, N.Y. in Early Photographs*, Vincent F. Seyfried and William Asadorian; and *Wild New York*, Margaret Mittelbach and Michael Crewdson.

The support of a number of individuals has gone a long way towards making this project a reality. My wife, Marilyn Albin Reichstein, developed the design concept, including choosing the type face, reviewing the photographs, and helping to prepare visuals to send to publishers. Steve Suckenik accompanied me on many field trips, adding both to the quality of the photography and the restaurant reviews as well as encouraging me to bring the book to the public's attention. Nancy Sonemann provided astute editing, I only wish I had taken her advice earlier. Barbara P. Trippel graciously proofread the manuscript. Laura Walworth provided major graphic and computer assistance, consolidating the various disks yielding the first complete draft of the book. John Henderson did a wonderful job in preparing the manuscript for production; and Nancy Feder who, early in the process, kindly provided computer assistance for the critical first chapters.

Steven Schechter of the MTA New York City Transit Authority was extremely helpful in providing transit information and travel times; his colleague, Joe Raskin, provided data on bus routes. A number of people in the Real Property Assessment Unit of the Queens Office of the New York City Department of Finance provided information regarding real estate market values, specifically Susan Lax, Mitch Ruben, Joseph Sprague, Martin Bernstein, Kevin Kelly, and Tom Keogh.

Also helpful were Susan Evans, Anita Harrison, Robert Hof, and Brian Nixon. I would also like to thank the President of the Borough of Queens, Claire Shulman, and the Deputy Borough President, Peter Magnani for their support. A number of other people provided suggestions and information that were helpful in the researching and writing of this book. Though I have failed to mention them by name, I am still indebted to them for their assistance.

Introduction

Now is the time for Queens to be discovered by:
■ People who live in Queens.
■ People who want to live in Manhattan, but can't afford to.
■ People who want to buy homes, condos, and co-ops in Queens.
■ People who live in high priced areas who are tired of the high cost.
■ People looking for new places to explore where they will not be bored.
■ People looking to try new restaurants, but only if the restaurants are good.

Many people who live in Queens do not know much about their borough outside of their own neighborhood. Most people who live outside of Queens know almost nothing about it. This book is an attempt to bring to the attention of residents and non-residents the many positive qualities that Queens possesses: some fine residential neighborhoods; half-a-hundred exceptionally good restaurants; unique museums; state-of-the-art performing arts centers; and easily accessible and plentiful recreational facilities.

Let's face it, Manhattan and much of Brooklyn are overpriced and offer too little space for too much money. It's different in Queens. The areas I've identified have interesting architecture, a sense of community, ample greenery, and are good values.

Schools are one of the prime reasons that families move to the suburbs that surround New York City. Yet there are many good, even outstanding, schools in Queens. This book provides information on both public and private schools in 28 residential areas. Elementary schools in all but five of the areas have reading scores in the top half of all public schools in the city. Seven public elementary schools mentioned in the book rank in the top 10 percent of all elementary schools in New York City.

There is another reason why Queens' reputation as a good place to live has remained: Queens was the first suburb of Manhattan that was built to accommodate and take advantage of the automobile. Compared to the other boroughs, Queens' neighborhoods have been less negatively affected by the automobile, while its superb highway system gives its residents an extraordinary amount of mobility

If Queens had a flag, green would be its color because of the vast parks the borough incorporates. Most of the neighborhoods mentioned in the book are near one or more large parks—parks of several hundred acres or more—as well as minutes from outdoor recreation facilities such as golf courses and tennis courts.

And restaurants in Queens reflect the new diversity of the borough. The food is genuinely ethnic and thoroughly original. Several upscale restaurants that now flourish in Manhattan first opened in Queens.

It should be noted, also, that owning residential property in New York City offers financial advantages that the surrounding suburbs don't offer. Real estate taxes on residential property in Queens are about one-third to one-half of what they are in most of the New York Metropolitan Area outside of New York City.

This book, with its 82 photographs, is designed to allow readers to get a feeling for each of the neighborhoods. The reader is also provided with a list of recommended restaurants, organized by type of cuisine. Finally, the reader is provided with descriptions of the most interesting places to visit in the borough, be they beach, museum, park, or other facility.

Format

The book consists of three major sections. The first lists the best restaurants in Queens and describes the food and the expected cost of a meal. Section two lists the best places to play in Queens. The major museums, performing arts theaters, interesting parks, tennis centers, golf courses, and other attractions are described. Section three consists of photographs and a description of 28 areas—all visually interesting—to live in in Queens. For each area there is an introduction, which summarizes the area's character and amenities, followed by subsections on *Real Estate, Transportation, Shopping, Education, Recreation.* Other specific information, relating to libraries, private schools, parochial schools, can be found in the Appendix at the back of the book.

A key aspect of this book is that it is purposefully organized. The areas are listed in alphabetical order. Within each area the subjects are listed in the same order and with the same format. This allows the reader readily to compare a particular subsection between different areas. If a neighborhood's price range is beyond the means of the reader, the reader can skim the *Real Estate* sections quickly to find an area that he or she can afford. If schools are a major concern, by looking at the *Education* section, the reader can compare the ranking and other information regarding schools in each area. If commuting to Manhattan is of importance, the *Transportation* section tells the reader how to get there and how long it will take by car, train, bus, or railroad.

Information Sources

Official government information forms the basis for all the subjects except for the *Shopping* section, which is based on the author's own surveys. Real Estate information was provided by the New York City Department of Finance. Transportation information on subways and buses was obtained from the Metropolitan Transportation Authority/New York City Transit; commuter train information came from the Long Island Rail Road; express bus information was provided by the New York City Department of Transportation, and the individual private bus lines. Education information was obtained from the New York City Board of Education. Library information was supplied by the Queens Public Library. Recreation data was obtained from source books of the New York City Department of Parks and Recreation. College cultural information was compiled from information supplied by the five colleges in Queens. All the restaurants listed were personally reviewed by me.

Queens has a lot to be proud of. Writing this book has been an adventure which helped me discover the treasures of the borough—its neighborhoods, its people, its food, and its architecture. I hope that this book will be a useful guide as well as a stimulus for readers to embark on a similar journey of discovery.

Contents

Where To Play In Queens

Where To Live In Queens

(which neighborhoods and which areas within them)

Appendix

.

History Of Development In Queens

Queens lies across the East River from Manhattan's East Side. It is the largest borough in New York City (112 square miles) and is four times the size of Manhattan. It has the most one- and two-family homes of any borough and accounts for 50 percent of all such homes in New York City. Almost square in shape—it's about fourteen miles from east to west and about fifteen miles from north to south—it occupies the space between the suburban towns and villages of Long Island (Nassau and Suffolk counties) and Manhattan's job, entertainment, and medical complexes. From its founding by English and Dutch settlers in the 1640's until little more than 100 years ago, Queens was a farming community with a few modest-sized towns and a scattering of communities started by real estate developers.

Climate, soil, and proximity to Manhattan shaped the early history of Queens. Queens has fertile soil and one of the longest growing seasons in the Northeastern United States—209 frost free days between mid-April and early November. The favorable conditions helped give rise to farms that grew the vegetables and fruit that fed much of the rapidly growing population of Manhattan. In 1850, after more than 200 years of settlement, the population of Queens was only 20,000.

Queens County had been carved out of western and central Long Island in 1683 and named after Catherine of Braganza, Queen of England, wife of Charles II. It was a big county; until 1898, it included what is now Nassau County and extended all the way to the Suffolk County border.

It remained primarily an agricultural area until after the Civil War when some industry began to develop and real estate developers, following the early railroad lines, began to buy land. Between the end of the Civil War and the turn of the century (1865-1900), real estate developments were started in such places as Woodside in 1867; Richmond Hill and Glendale in 1868; Astoria, Bayside, and South Flushing in 1872; and Ridgewood in 1881. But the early developers were ahead of their time. None of these early railroad suburbs grew rapidly or were densely developed. In 1900, Queens had a population of only 153,000.

Two events in the first decade of the 20th Century brought a rapid end to the borough's agricultural nature and led to a rapid increase in its population. In 1905 the Long Island Rail Road began electrified service and in 1909 the Queensboro Bridge opened and connected Queens to the burgeoning population of Manhattan. The electrification of the railroads and the new subway and rail tunnels built under the East River, especially the Long Island Rail Road tunnel connection to Pennsylvania Station completed in 1910, put the farmland of Queens within easy commuting distance of businesses and factories in Manhattan. Developers were quick to realize that, rather than grow fruits and vegetables, this land would be used more profitably to build homes for the people wishing to flee overcrowded Manhattan.

Auburndale was established in 1901; Stockholm Street in Ridgewood was started in 1905; Douglaston Manor, Forest Hills, Hollis Park Gardens, and Laurelton in 1906; Malba in 1908; Forest Hills Gardens and Kew Gardens in 1912; and Jackson Heights in 1913. Although the First World War broke out in 1914, the five-cent fare and the quick, reliable service provided by the subways continued to fuel a land development boom in Queens. By 1918, when the war was over, the subways had been extended as far as 168th Street in Jamaica. The 1920 Census listed the population of Queens at 469,000.

The 1920's saw the disappearance of almost all of the remaining farms as they and much of the remaining vacant land were converted to new residential developments. Addisleigh Park, Bowne Park, Sunnyside Gardens, and the Closes in Forest Hills were all developed in the 1920's. By 1930 the population of Queens stood at 1,079,000, a gain, on average, of approximately 60,000 people a year during the decade and a doubling of the population since 1920. A fabulous decade indeed.

The Depression of the 1930's brought the building boom in Queens to a halt. However, massive public works projects were started during the Depression that prepared the groundwork for further growth at the end of the Second World War in 1945. A system of highways was begun that provided high-speed access throughout the borough. Between 1933 and 1935 the Grand Central Parkway was completed to the Nassau County line and the Jackie Robinson Parkway (formerly known as the Interboro Parkway) connected Queens to Brooklyn. Both are car-only parkways and still prohibit trucks. Two great and beautiful bridges were built as part of the expanding highway network that serves Queens so efficiently today. The Triborough Bridge and the Whitestone Bridge were built in 1936 and 1939, respectively. The former connects Queens to Manhattan, the latter connects Queens to the Bronx. In 1940 the Cross Island Parkway, connecting the Whitestone Bridge on the north to the Belt Parkway in Brooklyn on the south, was built. And in 1940, the Midtown Tunnel opened, securely tying Queens to Manhattan.

A second major Queens building boom occurred between the late 1940's and the mid-1960's. Thousands of homes and apartments were constructed in eastern Queens, especially in Kew Gardens Hills, Fresh Meadows, Oakland Gardens, Glen Oaks, Holliswood, Bayside, Laurelton, Rosedale, and Springfield Gardens. The final links that make up the highway system also were finished during this period: The Van Wyck Expressway in 1950, the Long Island Expressway in the late 1950's, the Clearview Expressway and Throgs Neck Bridge in 1961, and the Brooklyn-Queens Expressway in 1962.

Since the 1970's Queens—known primarily as an almost homogeneous bedroom community of Manhattan—has seen changes that have given rise to several diverse communities with interesting, individual identities. These changes have provided rich opportunities for those inclined to experience the type of stores, restaurants, and entertainment usually found only in Manhattan. Other than at the United Nations, more languages are spoken in Queens than in any other borough. Today, the Borough of Queens provides a superior level-of-living environment within the metropolitan area, enriched by distinctive architecture, historic districts, and pockets of ethnic diversity.

Where To Eat In Queens

RESTAURANTS: A WONDERLAND OF DIVERSE CUISINES

The restaurants in Queens surprise people. Service is friendlier, prices are lower, and when it comes to ethnic food—Greek, Chinese, Indian, Malaysian, Korean, Latin American—it's often better than in the hyped world of Manhattan. This shouldn't be surprising, since restaurants are an organic part of the ethnic neighborhoods of Queens. This is where the Chinese eat Chinese food, the Greeks eat Greek food, and the Koreans eat Korean food. Food in these restaurants is authentic and good. Queens, by the way, is the most ethnically diverse of the City's boroughs; at least 178 languages are spoken.

Most of the more popular restaurants are concentrated in fewer than a half-dozen areas: Astoria (Greek and Italian), Flushing (Chinese, Malaysian, Korean), Jackson Heights (Latin American, Indian), Forest Hills (Cajun/Creole, Continental, Italian, Thai, Brick-Oven Pizza), and Rego Park (Chinese and Seafood). Many other restaurants worth a visit are located throughout the borough.

The following 50 restaurants (there are over 2,500 in Queens, ranging from fast food to eye-popping romantic) are my top choices. All of these restaurants are either good, very good, or excellent in what they do. Many of them have been favorably reviewed in newspapers, such as *The New York Times,* and guides, such as *Zagat.* All of them should provide an enjoyable dining experience. The price shown is the approximate cost of an average dinner (three courses, where appropriate), excluding drinks, but including tax and tip.

AMERICAN

Water's Edge, 44th Drive and East River (Long Island City): (718) 482-0033. Very good food in a romantic setting facing the East River, Roosevelt Island, and the United Nations. Prix fixe lunches at $20 and $29; prix fixe dinners at $60, $75, and $85, excluding tax and tip. The $85 dinner is five courses and includes wine with each course. Food is expertly prepared and handsomely presented. Entrees include: poached red snapper, Chilean sea bass, monkfish, scallops, Alaskan char, smoked duck, pan fried pork filet, grilled veal chops, roast beef, and short ribs. Tasty vegetable side dishes. Interesting appetizers. Attentive service.

ARGENTINIAN

La Fusta, 80-32 Baxter Avenue (Elmhurst): (718) 429-8222. Very good—go for the beef. For your entrée, try entrana, grilled skirt steak. It's tender and tasty, like filet mignon. Appetizers are varied, but the meats are best. Try moricilla (blood sausage) and matambre (slices of cold roast beef wrapped around slices of hard boiled egg with mixed olives and Russian salad on the side. There is a large menu that includes a variety of grilled meat, pasta, empenadas, and fish dishes. The red house wine is good and inexpensive; desserts are appealing. The restaurant is unpretentious, the service decent. A tavern is next door. $30

La Portena, 74-25 37th Avenue (Jackson Heights): (718) 458-8111. Good grilled skirt steak, tasty blood sausage, and excellent mussels provençal are some of the dishes served with pride at this small, colorful, photo-covered, wood-walled, and beamed-ceiling establishment. The flan, with dollops of soft, dark caramel on the side, is delicious. Pasta dishes are also available. Good service. $25

BOLIVIAN

Nostaligias, 85-09 Northern Boulevard (Jackson Heights): (718) 533-9120. Good. A somewhat different type of South American cuisine: some bland dishes, some dishes with a hot salsa on the side. Best for Friday and Saturday dining when there are a number of specials. Start with an appetizer such as saltenas, small, delicious chicken or beef pies. Then try a soup, there are several, such as peanut soup, potato and white corn soup, and especially delicious soups only made on the weekend. Ask for them. Entrées include: chicken, shredded beef, tongue, roast pork. Entrées are usually accompanied by one or more of the following: potatoes, rice, onions, roasted banana, sweet potato, or corn. There is flan for dessert. Good service. Karaoke on weekends at 10:00 p.m. $25

BRAZILIAN

Master Grill, 34-09 College Point Boulevard (Flushing): (718) 762-0300. Good, if you enjoy an all-you-can-eat buffet, featuring a dozen or more varieties of grilled meats, such as sausage, chicken, turkey, beef ribs, duck, beef, lamb shish-kebab, rib-eye, pork loin, skirt steak, filet mignon, suckling pig. Save room for the last four dishes—they are the best. And there's more—a buffet of different salads and at least 10 hot side dishes. The mussels, spare ribs, and fried bananas stood out. Banquet-room size with showy decor. A band plays every evening. Good service. Valet parking. Dinner $25 (lunch served 12 to 3 is about $8 less). Gratuity included in the price.

BUKHARIAN (ASIAN RUSSIAN)

Salute, 63-42 108th Street (Forest Hills): (718) 275-6860. Good home-style food at a reasonable price in a small, pleasant, kosher restaurant. Pickled appetizers, soups, shish-kebabs, pilav, and dumplings are featured. The soups are fresh, filling, and tasty, whether with noodles and small pieces of meat or with pasta and vegetables. The chicken shish-kebabs are standouts, and the Crimean pastries filled with beef (cheburekes) and the large noodle-dough dumplings filled with bits of lamb, onions, and sweet spices (Uzbek Mantu) are delicious. The green tea is flavorful and non-astringent. The desserts are good, especially the walnut-and-sugar squares and the crème puff pastry. Attentive service. Kosher. $20

CAJUN/CREOLE

Cooking With Jazz, 12-01 154th Street (Whitestone): (718) 767-6979. Very good New Orleans style food. The space is small, pleasant, and unusual; the food is unquestionably worth the trip. Blackened fish coated with spices, chicken jambalaya, chicken with mouth-watering buttermilk biscuits, and shrimp and crayfish dishes are all good. There are also non-Cajun dishes for those who like things mild. Appetizers and side dishes, such as garlic mashed potatoes, are good. So are the cornbread and the desserts—try the sweet potato pie. Attentive service. $35

Mardi Gras, 70-20 Austin Street (Forest Hills): (718) 261-8555. Good New Orleans style food in lively, loud, music-filled surroundings. The cooking is surprisingly good in this little bit of New Orleans on Austin Street. The crowd is young and the noise level high, but the gumbo, blackened fish and meats, crawfish, ribs, shrimp creole, and of course jambalaya are all available. The appetizers, such as cajun crawfish popcorn, catfish bites, alligator pops are lightly battered, fried and mouth-watering—not at all heavy or greasy. The blackened catfish is light, moist, and nicely spiced. Try the side dishes such as sweet potato fries—rich and satisfying. Desserts are interesting and well presented. Service is friendly, but genuine Cajun cooking takes time. $30

CARIBBEAN

Cabana, 107-10 70th Road (Forest Hills): (718) 263-3600. Good food with a Spanish Caribbean emphasis. Start with an appetizer like baccalaitos, four, thin, lightly fried codfish cakes with a wonderful, mild avocado salsa between each cake; or try, conch, jerk chicken wings, plantains, or Jamaican empanadas filled with spicy beef. The coco cabana chicken entrée is very good. It is made with chunks of chicken cooked in a coconut milk curry with West Indian pumpkin, yucca, potatoes, and carrots. A small mound of rice is placed in the center of the dish. Delicious. There are also about a dozen other entrees, including churrasco, a skirt steak; paraillada, a mixed meat grill; paella;

shrimps in garlic sauce; and boneless sauteed chicken breasts. Interesting desserts, such as banana fritters, pastry turnovers filled with passion fruit puree, mango ice cream, and of course, flan. Decent service. $30

COLOMBIAN

Tierras Colombianas, 33-01 Broadway (Astoria): (718) 956-3012. Good, hearty food in informal, sometimes noisy, dining room (choose the enclosed sidewalk dining room, instead). Food is plentiful and flavorful. Main dishes such as pork chops, barbecued ribs, shrimp scampi, and fish dishes are standouts. The rice, beans, and sweet plantains are also good. Courteous service. $20

CHINESE

Golden Monkey, 133-47 Roosevelt Avenue (Flushing): (718) 762-2664. Very good Sichuan food, varying from mild to hot. A favorite dish of customers and the house is steamed sea bass with small cubes of bean curd, diced scallions, and flecks of red peppers in a special sauce. The fish is white, light and tasty, while the sauce provides a tangy counterpoint. The Chinese vegetables are prepared well; there are non-spicy dishes, too, such as crispy duck with taro and plum sauce. No desserts. This is a simple, but pleasant, basement restaurant with friendly, helpful service. $25

Goody's, 94-03B 63rd Drive (Rego Park): (718) 896-7163. Good Shanghai food. Excellent "soup buns" filled with pork, and soup, delicious turnip rolls and tofu in brown sauce. Large portions (you'll take food home), basic décor, and helpful waiters. $20

Joe's Shanghai, 136-21 37th Avenue (Flushing): (718) 539-3838. Very good. The steamed crabmeat dumplings are fantastic and alone are worth the trip. The many other, typical Chinese dishes are good, especially the fish dishes, but nothing compares to the crabmeat dumplings. Basic décor. Very popular and busy. $20

K.B. Garden, 136-28 39th Avenue (Flushing): (718) 961-9088. Very good dim sum lunch. Large selection of these small platters to enjoy and share. Especially good are: clams in brown sauce, tasty and nicely spiced; barbecued pieces of spare ribs in garlic sauce; shrimp balls encased in a translucent rice dough; and vegetable dumplings filled with a mixture of green Chinese vegetables. Located on the second floor, the large, open, high ceilinged dining room is pleasant, if a bit glitzy. The helpful waitresses can usually explain the contents of each dish. Ample parking. $15

Laifood, 38-18 Prince Street (Flushing): (718) 321-0653. Good Taiwanese food. Best bet is the tasty, hot pot/casserole in winter, for two-to-four people. The steaming hot broth is filled with a variety of fish, shellfish, and fish balls. Some dishes are an acquired taste, such as several featuring innards. Small, simple dining rooms. $25

Ping's, 83-02 Queens Boulevard (Elmhurst): (718) 396-1238. Good, absolutely fresh fish, crabs (including Dungeness), lobsters, and shrimp, served in a variety of dishes with the sauces made to suit individual tastes. The bean curd and several varieties of greens are quite good. Nice presentation. Good service includes hot hand towels. Pleasant ambience. $25

Shanghai Tang, 135-20 40th Road (Flushing): (718) 661-4234. Very good, especially dumplings, appetizers, such as turnip rolls, and many of the noodle dishes. Polite, courteous service. Pleasant décor and ambience. You may even want to linger over tea and orange slices. $20

Silver Pond, 56-50 Main Street @ 56th Avenue (Flushing): (718) 463-2888. Very good seafood; good for dim sum. Large, open dining room. Pleasantly decorated. Dishes are good and presented well. $20

CONTINENTAL/MEDITERRANEAN

Bistro Metro, 107-21 Metropolitan Avenue (Forest Hills): (718) 263-5444. Very good, upscale restaurant. Eastern Mediterranean appetizers are featured, but there are also eclectic dishes such as: sauteed portobello mushrooms; seared blackened tuna sushi with ginger and wasabi; homemade zucchini cakes with sour cream; three mousse combination of chickpeas, eggplant, and caviar; and half-portions of ravioli or fettuccine with various sauces. The entrees include salmon; swordfish; halibut; prawns; scallops or filet mignon in merlot sauce; shell steak with shallots; a rack of three lamb chops; and a vegetarian entrée of grilled vegetables. The roast duck with a raspberry glaze is tender, meaty, and covered with a crisp skin that is a wonderful foil to this rich tasting dish. Desserts include cheese cake, tarts, key lime pie, and sorbet. Good service. $45

ECUADORIAN

Galapagos ll, 91-17 37th Avenue (Jackson Heights): (718) 429-5657. Very good, storefront-style neighborhood restaurant with a palm tree mural. Food is fresh, tasty, and different. For an appetizer try ceviche mixto pequeno, a chilled mixture of cooked fish, octopus, and shrimp marinated in a tangy sauce. Goat dishes are a recommended entrée. So is the sopa marinera, a mixture of crab, mussels, clams, and fish in a rich, delicious, flavorful broth—there is enough for two. No desserts, but the local drinks are fun and good. Try lulo, a frothy mixture of lime juice, sugar, and water; or avena/quaker, an oat and clove drink that is surprisingly refreshing. Helpful service, but minimal English. $15

GERMAN

Gebhardt's, 65-06 Myrtle Avenue (Glendale): (718) 821-5567. Good German food in a warm, subdued setting. The noise level is low—it's a good place for conversation. The food is fresh and the portions are generous. Appetizers include several herring dishes, fresh suelze (head cheese), and chopped liver. All are tasty and good. Entrées include sauerbraten, schnitzels, loin of pork, filet of pork, steaks, and half-a-dozen seafood dishes. The side dishes of red cabbage, potato dumplings, and sauerkraut are all quite good. Try bauernschmaus, also known as farmer's delight. It contains most of the German menu: succulent loin of pork, satisfying knockwurst, tender pot roast, light dumplings; mild sauerkraut, and a crispy potato pancake complete with apple sauce. There is apple strudel, butterscotch sundaes, and ice cream for dessert. Service is attentive. Sit and chat. No one is rushing you out. $30

Zum Stammtisch, 69-46 Myrtle Avenue (Glendale): (718) 386-3014. Very good German food in pleasant, high-ceilinged, inn-like setting. The name of the restaurant means family table, and the background sound is that of polkas and light-hearted songs. Two dining rooms, one for smokers. Excellent German beers on tap. Good food with large portions; lots of doggie bags were evident. Appetizers include several herring dishes, head cheese, pickled beef with onions, and smoked brook trout with creamed horseradish. The goulash soup, loaded with tiny pieces of meat, is almost a meal in itself. The house specialty is Jagerschnitzel, lightly breaded veal cutlet covered with a mushroom sauce and lightly seasoned. There are also good wursts, sauerbraten, and daily specials, such as loin of pork and duck. Rich desserts, including coffee with liqueur and whipped cream. Attentive service. $35

GREEK

Christos Hasapo-Taverna, 41-08 23rd Avenue (Astoria): (718) 726-5195. Good Greek steakhouse in realistic turn-of the-century tavern setting. Dark wood, light walls, old photos, and memorabilia add to the charm. A small meat counter offers meats for sale. The tarama (fish roe puree) and melitzano (eggplant salad) are good, as are the filet mignon and lamb chops. The galaktoboureko, for dessert, is a winner. $30

Elias Corner, 24-02 31st Street (Astoria): (718) 932-1510. Good Greek fish restaurant. Popular and busy. Basic décor. The appetizers are quite good, especially the fish roe (tarama); the salads are large, fresh, tasty and not over dressed; the fish dishes are huge and taste just caught: you'll take food home. No desserts. $25

Karyatis, 35-03 Broadway (Astoria): (718) 204-0666. Excellent Greek food in upscale setting; warm ambience and good service. Music on Saturday nights. The appetizers are delicious, whether cold or hot—you can make a meal by ordering several.

Especially good are the cold and the hot combination platters that let you sample four appetizers at a time. The fish entrees are good, as are the meat dishes. Good house wine. It's easy to order too much. $35

Nostalgia Taverna, 34-12 Broadway (Astoria): (718) 726-4500. Very good Greek dishes and Cyprian specialties. There are more than a dozen appetizers to choose from, such as crabcakes, Greek sausage, and sweetbreads. The taramasalata, a tangy fish roe spread and the octopus are especially good. Entrées are typical of what you would expect in a Greek restaurant, but they are prepared to perfection. The moussaka is creamy, light, and excellent. The spinach pie is light, flaky and very good. The side dishes, such as potatoes or dandelion greens are prepared with care–they are neither oily nor overdone. The menu has many grilled dishes, such as chicken souvlaki, swordfish, lambchops, shrimps, and a fish of the day. Stuffed dishes include cabbage, chicken, and leg of lamb. The ambience is pleasant and unpretentious. Sevice is good. $25

S'Agapo, 34-21 34th Avenue (Astoria): (718) 626-0303. Very good Greek and Cretan dishes. Start with pikilia orektikon, a platter of cold dips and spreads that includes: hummos, roasted eggplant, piquant grape leaves, fish roe, roasted red peppers, yogurt with cucumbers, and a tart parsley spread. There are many delicious hot appetizers, such as the spinach pastry. For the entrée, fish, such as porgy, is highly recommended. Tasty side dishes: dandelion, rice, potatoes. Desserts include a good galaktoboureko, a cake made of filo dough and custard, and giaourti me meli, a Cretan specialty of thickened yogurt, honey, and nuts. Pleasant ambience, well-spaced tables. Polite, attentive service. $35

Taverna Vraka, 23-15 31st Street (Astoria): (718) 721-3007. Excellent Greek and Cyprian food in upscale setting. Begin with the cold and/or hot appetizers—both are quite good. Try a combination plate with fish roe, eggplant, and three types of cheese: feta, kaseri, and halloumi—a slightly salty cheese from Cyprus. Everything is amazingly fresh and tastes homemade. The generous platter of octopus was tender and tasty. Two particularly wonderful entrees are striped bass topped with onions and minced tomato—sweet and succulent—and baked lamb and artichokes—the baking does for the artichokes what it does for garlic, the flavor is sweeter, the consistency delightful. The desserts are good. There is a good red house wine. The ambience is comfortable and pleasant, but it gets lively when the music begins at 9:00 p.m. Service is excellent, gracious and attentive. $40

INDIAN

Delhi Palace, 37-33 74th Street (Jackson Heights): (718) 507-0666. Excellent Indian food, well prepared. Two excellent dishes are: saag gosht, succulent cubes of lamb buried in a wonderfully flavored, spiced-spinach puree; and lamb biryani, nicely flavored rice combined with minced vegetables and topped with strips of lamb. Also try: the dhal, a spicy thick sauce made of lentils; the plain or mango lassi drink, and for dessert, either gulab jamun—two sweet balls of pastry covered with syrup; or semiyan—very liquid form of rice pudding consisting of rendered milk, nuts, raisins, and vermicelli. A large mural adorns the walls. Attentive service. $20

Jackson Diner, 37-47 74th Street (Jackson Heights): (718) 672-1232. Excellent Indian food from a variety of different regions. There are mild dishes, such as vegetable tandoori, chicken tandoori, aloo gobi—potatoes and cauliflower mixed with masala—and dal makhani—lentils and kidney beans with tomatoes, ginger, and coriander. There are good spicy dishes as well: hot broiled eggplant and onions; chickpeas and diced potatoes in a punjabi sauce; and many specials, featuring lamb, goat, or chicken prepared in various curries, herbs, and sauces. Try a lassi—a delightful yogurt beverage that's ideal for restoring the palate after a spicy dish. The mango lassi is exceptional. This large, spacious, and pleasant restaurant, with its adequate service, exceptionally fresh, reasonably priced, and well prepared food, is very popular with anyone who likes Indian food. $15

ITALIAN

Parkside, 107-01 Corona Avenue at 51st Avenue (Corona): (718) 271-9276. Good traditional Italian food accompanied by excellent service, from tuxedo clad waiters, in pleasant dining rooms overflowing with live plants. There are many appetizers to choose from. Two of the best are a delicious hot antipasto consisting of stuffed clams, stuffed zucchini, mushrooms, and jumbo shrimp; and an exquisitely tender, nicely seasoned and stuffed artichoke. The entrees, whether veal, fish, or pasta were tasty and well presented. The breadbasket contained first-rate rolls and delicious varieties of bread. Desserts include several types of good-tasting tarts. There is complimentary biscotti. Valet parking. $35

Piccola Venezia, 42-01 28th Avenue (Astoria): (718) 721-8470. Excellent food emphasizing Northern Italian cooking. This three-decade-old establishment has some of the best Italian food served anywhere. While it has a wide selection of the usual entrées, including pasta, fish, and veal, its preparation of even "standard" dishes is creative, visually appealing, and delicious. The gnocchi, tiny, light potato dumplings, covered with a piquant, creamy gorgonzola sauce is delightful; as is the pasta fusi alla grappa, bowtie-shaped pasta with a sauce of muchrooms, grappa, and parmigiano. The soup pasta e fagioli is a classic; the veal dishes, such as on the bone veal chop, are quite good; but the duck in a rich Grand Marnier sauce is outstanding. The desserts are delectable. The flan-like pannacotta is smooth, creamy, and light; the pistachio cannoli is an inspired creation. All the desserts are artfully presented. Attentive service from a caring, helpful staff. The two dining rooms are comfortable, subdued, and relatively quiet. Valet parking. $55

Trattoria L'incontro, 21-76 31st Street (Astoria): (718) 721-3532. Good food with Northern Italian accent. This bright, new restaurant has a high ceiling, modern ambience, and pleasant décor. A tasty spread of pureed, sun-dried tomatoes, olive oil, and a bit of garlic, is provided with the bread. Don't worry if you eat it all—another will appear. The many daily specials have mouth-watering ingredients—the waiters will gladly repeat the selections if you can't make up your mind. There are a wide variety of dishes, ranging from a dozen different pastas in delicious sauces to several well made veal dishes to individual brick oven pizzas. The food is freshly prepared and well presented. Desserts are rich and good. Valet parking is available in the evening. Unfortunately, the food and service are uneven on the weekends when there tend to be large and noisy parties. $35

JAPANESE

Narita, 107-08 70th Road (Forest Hills): (718) 263-2999. Good food in a pleasant setting. This subdued, but upscale, restaurant is located in Forest Hills' restaurant row. The attentive and helpful staff can easily guide you through the extensive menu. Sushi, sashimi, maki, teriyaki, tempura, and noodle dishes in broth are some of the more familiar items. Especially good is the miso soup, the chicken teriyaki, and the vegetable and shrimp tempura. The green tea is robust. An interesting touch for dessert is Japanese ice cream: the green tea and the red bean flavors actually complement the meal, seem less fattening, and are worth trying. There is a tatami mat seating area; a teppanaki/ hibachi area; and a regular seating area with tables for two to four persons. The food is presented quite nicely in attractive compartmentalized trays. There is a small bar. $30

KOREAN

Dae Dong, 46-07 Queens Boulevard (Sunnyside): (718) 482-7100. Good, spicy food cooked on a grill at your table. Strips of marinated meat or fish are fun to coat with delicious, pungent sauces and barbecue on your own. The traditional Korean side dishes of kimchi (pickled vegetables, especially cabbage) are quite good, as are the scallion pancakes. Helpful waiters. Korean motif. $25

Kum Gang San, 138-28 Northern Boulevard (Flushing): (718) 461-0909. Good Korean food can be ordered from a large menu that includes pictures of most of the dishes. The main dishes are prepared in numerous variations, such as steamed rice topped with shrimps, mussels, scallops, squid, mild green and red peppers, and olive oil. It is served sizzling in an individual stoneware pot. There also are grilled beef, fish, and poultry selections, as well as the famous side dishes for which the cuisine is noted: bean sprouts, steamed spinach, thinly sliced strips of radish, crunchy seaweed, a very fishy fish vermircelli, spicy cabbage, tofu, and vegetable greens. In addition, the meal includes a smoky and delicious mini-bowl of rice porridge, a bowl of miso soup, and a plate of fruit for dessert. Open 24-hours. Japanese dishes are served, also. There is a sushi bar. Helpful service. The décor is Asian, with lots of wood and a small waterfall. $20

KOSHER *(see also: Bukharian-Asian Russian)*

Ben's Bayside Kosher Delicatessen, 211-37 26 Avenue (Bayside): (718) 229-2967. Located in the Clearview Shopping Center. Good, authentic Jewish delicatessen. It's usually busy and can be noisy. But it's clean, modern, and the deli, pickles, and cream soda make it worth it. $15

MALAYSIAN

Penang, 38-04 Prince Street (Flushing): (718) 321-2078. Very good. This is the modest storefront restaurant that launched its popular, upscale, Manhattan sibling. The roti, satays, and noodle dishes, especially the ones featuring shrimp or seafood, are all good. Taro dishes are tasty and suitable for those who don't like things too spicy. Busy. Service is good. $20

MEXICAN

Sgt. Garcia, 70-09 Austin Street (Forest Hills): (718) 575-0007. Good Mexican food that has been made a bit gentle for the American taste. If you want it hotter, just tell the waiter. Ingredients are fresh and the dishes are nicely presented. The usual standbys—fajitas, enchiladas, burritos—are all tasty, as are the rice and refried beans. The black bean soup is rich and hearty, a bowl is almost a meal in itself; scallops in red wine sauce is a wonderful appetizer—ask for bread to sop up the sauce. The large menu includes grilled meats, fish, many shrimp dishes, chili, Mexican beers, tequila and a large selection of wines. The décor is pleasant, but modest—wood floors, simulated wood formica tables. Service is good. The weekend evening crowd is lively. $25

PERUVIAN

Inti Raymi, 86-14 37th Avenue (Jackson Heights): (718) 424-1938. Good, small, but long established restaurant with a large selection of tasty dishes to choose from, some quite spicy. The anticuches are tender slices of veal heart served on a skewer. The entrée arroz verde con mariscos, consisting of green (cilantro) rice, scallops, shrimp, calamari, clams, mussels, and octopus, is very good. The desserts, besides three variations of flan, also include an excellent mazamorra, a slightly sweet, slightly jellied, cranberry color corn and fruit dish with a taste that belies its ingredients. The alfajores—a cookie made with sugar, caramel and condensed milk—is nice, also. Helpful service. Whitewashed walls, wood paneling, Inca motif. Open Thursday through Sunday. $25

Pio Pio, 84-13 Northern Boulevard (Jackson Heights): (718) 426-1010. Very good. This is the place to go for tender, moist, tasty, roast chicken—it's cooked on a spit.

They had better do it well—it's the only entrée! However, combine this with an excellent appetizer (that can feed four), such as ensalada de mariscos, consisting of squid, mussels, octopus, shrimp, and pieces of fish, nicely presented on a bed of lettuce, with dressing, and you have a bounteous and delicious meal. There are also side dishes of rice, beans, plantains. And don't forget the flan. The ambience is modern, yet warm. Good service. Specials on Sundays before 4. $20

PORTUGUESE

O Lavrador, 138-40 101st Avenue (Richmond Hill): (718) 526-1526. Good food, generous portions. Cozy dining room. Good appetizers are shrimp with garlic sauce and pork with potato. The collard green and potato soup is also quite good. The entrée, seafood mariscada, is a winner; the barbecued chicken is good. The green wine is excellent, inexpensive, and should be tried. Two types of flan for dessert, both good. Reasonable service. $25

PIZZA /BRICK-OVEN

Dee's, 104-02 Metropolitan Avenue (Forest Hills): (888) 488-3337. Good brick-oven pizza. Several good appetizers to enjoy as you await your pizza: giant cooked beans in sauce, and eggplant salad are but two. Pasta, salad, dessert, and wine are available. Popular and informal. The restaurant can be noisy at peak times. $20

Nick's, 108-26 Ascan Avenue (Forest Hills): (718) 263-1126. Good brick-oven pizza. This small, plain storefront restaurant concentrates on pizza, but also offers a few salads. Popular. Noisy at times. $15

SEAFOOD

London Lennie's, 63-88 Woodhaven Boulevard (Rego Park): (718) 894-8064. Very good, expertly prepared fish dishes. Try the fish soups and bisques, fresh oysters and clams, crab cakes, and of course the fish, especially the fish of the day. Good desserts, such as key lime pie and cheesecake. Large, comfortable, and popular. Come early to get a table. $30

SPANISH

Café Salamanca, 79-05 Northern Boulevard (Jackson Heights): (718) 458-2446. Good Spanish food served in a charming, airy setting. Start with the free appetizer of three mussels cooked with minced onions and garlic; soups, such as caldo gallego (a mixture of white beans, diced potatoes, collard greens, and Spanish sausage) are delicious. Entrees include meat, fish, and poultry dishes. The old standby, paella Valenciana, is done well—sausages are especially tasty. Service is good. The small, modern bar allows smoking; you may want to sit in the back. $25

THAI

Q, a Thai Bistro, 108-25 Ascan Avenue near Austin Street (Forest Hills): (718) 261-6599. Excellent upscale Thai restaurant. The food is beautifully presented in an intimate setting. The Q features three-dozen good wines available by the glass, as well as many varieties of beer, and mixed drinks. Excellent appetizers include Thai vegetable roll with an exceptional tamarind sauce on the side, and dumplings that are light and delicious. There are also satays, grilled strips of meat marinated in herbs and coconut milk and served with peanut sauce and cucumber salad. The entrees are equally good and include: Phad Thai, rice noodles, shrimp, eggs, bean sprouts, and peanuts all mixed together, emanating wonderful aromas—the shrimp are delicious; Phad Si Eau, stir-fried rice noodles with chicken or beef and Chinese broccoli; and seared chicken breasts wrapped in crushed walnuts and cooked with peppers—a delicious dish that comes with mashed sweet potato, bok choy, thin strips of carrot, and a portion of rice ensconced in its own woven basket container. It's all almost too good-looking to eat. Other menu selections include: shrimp, red snapper, salmon, stir fried beef, filet mignon, and chicken. Attentive service. $35

Ubol's Kitchen, 24-42 Steinway Street (Astoria): (718) 545-2874. Very good assortment of Thai dishes ranging from lightly to hotly spiced. The modest storefront décor belies the delicious food and attentive, friendly service that seems to draw many young, ethnically mixed couples. Start with the flavorful jasmine tea, then choose from a large selection of appetizers: chicken satay with peanut sauce on the side and marvelously light vegetable dumplings are two of many good choices. There is an extensive selection of entrées: including duck, fishball specialties of frogs, shrimp, fish, and squid, familiar noodle dishes, such as pad thai, vegetable dishes, and chicken, pork, and beef dishes in various curries and sauces—red curry, green curry, ginger, and more. The Thai custard is an excellent dessert choice to overcome the meal's spices—it's like a fine bread pudding, but made with taro and coconut milk—not too plain and not too sweet. $20

TUNISIAN—FRENCH

La Baraka, 255-09 Northern Boulevard (Little Neck): (718) 428-1461. Very good Tunisian versions of a select list of French dishes. Soups, quite good, especially the onion; delicious fish dishes, such as sole; tasty shish kebabs. Excellent Turkish coffee; tempting, well presented desserts. $35

TURKISH

Kazan Turkish Cuisine, 95-36 Queens Boulevard (Rego Park): (718) 897-1509. Good food in inviting, light, and airy dining room. Quiet. Start with the scrumptious bread, just the right thing to munch as you sample the cold appetizer plate (containing eight items)—almost a meal in itself for two. All the appetizers are good, especially: hummus, eggplant dishes, yogurt dishes, white beans, fish roe, grape leaves, spinach and mixed chopped vegetables blended with Turkish spices. Two entrees worth trying are the kuzu shish yogurtlu: grilled chunks of lamb on a bed of crisp croutons covered with a zesty yogurt sauce; and kasarli kofte: small patties of chopped lamb sitting atop a moist rice pilaf pungent with Turkish spices. Kazandibi, a flat type of flan, makes a good dessert. Attentive service. Vegetarian dishes available. BYOB. $25

Where To Play In Queens

BASEBALL STADIUMS

Shea Stadium, 126th Street and Roosevelt Avenue: (718) 507-8499. Home of the New York Mets baseball team. Easily accessible by Number 7 train, Willets Point Station, or by car from the Grand Central Parkway, Long Island Expressway, or Van Wyck Expressway.

BEACHES

Rockaway Beach, on the Atlantic Ocean from Beach First Street in Far Rockaway to Beach 149th Street in Neponsit: (718) 318-4000. The beach is 7.5 miles long, city owned-and-operated, and easily accessible by car from Cross Bay Boulevard or by the IND subway A line. A boardwalk parallels a section of the beach and is open year-round. After 149th Street, the beach continues as part of Jacob Riis Park (718) 318-4300.

Jones Beach State Park: (516) 785-1600. While this beach is not in Queens, it is closer in travel-time to Queens than it is to any of the other boroughs. Most parts of Queens are less than 45 minutes by car from this beautiful Long Island beach, with its clean, soft, white sand, well maintained facilities, many life guard stations, ample parking, small boardwalk, and fine restaurant. The Park offers not only ocean swimming and surfing, but bay swimming as well.

COLLEGES AND CULTURAL OFFERINGS

Colleges play an important role in providing entertainment and culture to Queens residents. There are five colleges in Queens: LaGuardia Community College, Queens College, Queensboro Community College, St. John's University, and York College. They are all 30 minutes or less from any of the 28 neighborhoods listed. The approximate number of continuing education course offerings at each college, their areas of emphasis, available recreational facilities, and a sample of the college's cultural offerings are listed below. Access by mass transit is also noted.

La Guardia Community College, 31-10 Thomson Avenue: (718) 482-7200. Approximately 100 continuing education, multi-session courses are offered each term in a wide variety of subjects ranging from art to telecommunications. Special emphasis is put on computer courses, programs for children and teens, courses training adults for employment, English as a second language, and programs for deaf adults. There is a modern swimming pool and a state-of-the-art fitness center. Cultural offerings are presented in the LaGuardia Performing Arts Center's Mainstage Theatre, which seats 742, and the Little Theatre, which seats 210. Offerings include plays and dances geared to children and families. There is a parking garage and a parking lot nearby, as well as on-street parking. LaGuardia is accessible by subway from the E, F, G, N, and R train stops at Queens Plaza and Queensborough Plaza stations (an eight-minute walk to the main building) and the 7 train which stops at the Rawson Street Station (a three-minute walk). Three buses serve the college: the Q60, and Q32 along Queens Boulevard, and the Q39 from Ridgewood.

Queens College, 65-30 Kissena Boulevard: (718) 997-5000. Founded in 1937 as one of the senior colleges of the City of New York, the college offers approximately 200 continuing education, multi-session courses. Course offerings range from career training to personal development. Emphasis is placed on courses in business management, computers, health-related fields, real estate, paralegal studies, academic skills, and the arts and humanities. The college has a large, indoor swimming pool, a gym, and tennis courts. Queens College offers the largest number of cultural events available in the borough through the Colden Center for the Performing Arts, comprised of the 1,500-seat Colden Auditorium, the beautiful, 489-seat LeFrak Auditorium, and the 476-seat Queens College Theater. There are concert series, recitals, chamber music, jazz, pop specials, choral music, dance, and programs for family fun, as well as theatre for children. Internationally famous soloists regularly appear at the Colden Center. Six bus lines—the Q17, Q34, Q44, Q65A, Q74, Q88, and the Q25—stop at the main gate, or nearby. There is free public parking on campus.

Queensborough Community College, 222-05 56th Avenue: (718) 631-6262. The campus was constructed between 1967 and 1977 on 34 acres of the former Oakland Golf Course. Approximately 200 continuing education, multi-session courses are taught each semester in about 30 different areas of interest, ranging from business and investing to computers and interior design. The two largest programs are physical fitness, with about 50 courses, and a learning center for children with about 30 courses, not including additional courses for children in the areas of music and recreation. The college has an Olympic-size pool and a gym, both of which are open to the public. Cultural offerings are presented in several settings: the QCC Theater, which seats 875 and features professional troupes doing opera, folk ballet, and musicals, as well as professional orchestral and choral productions; the Kurzweil Recital Hall, which seats 90 and features piano concerts and small musical ensembles; the Little Theater, which seats 70 and presents plays performed by students; the Art Gallery, which mounts several exhibitions during the year;

and the Library Basement, which features films, forums, and discussion groups. There is free parking on campus. The College is also accessible by bus: the Q27, Q12, or Q30.

St. John's University, Union Turnpike and 173rd Street: (718) 990-6161. Founded in 1870, the University began to relocate from Brooklyn to Queens in 1955. In 1995, the University established a new academic unit—Metropolitan College—which sponsors a variety of programs with day, evening, and weekend time schedules. More than 120 multi-session courses are taught each term, ranging from the arts to sports. Two areas of emphasis are professional development and personal enrichment. An indoor swimming pool, gym, and weight room are used in teaching sport courses, such as scuba diving, yoga, and physical fitness. Cultural offerings of the University make use of the 611-seat Marillac Auditorium and the 450-seat Little Theatre where the Chappel Players of St. John's perform plays that are open to the public. There is free, public parking on campus. Three bus lines-—the Q30, Q31, and Q46—stop at the campus.

York College, 94-20 Guy R. Brewer Boulevard: (718) 262-2000. Built in 1983, it is the newest four-year college in Queens. Approximately 70 continuing education, multi-session courses are taught each term, with courses in academic skills, and computer studies, and several courses in child care training. An indoor swimming pool and a gym are available to the public. Cultural offerings are presented in the 1,500-seat Performing Arts Center Theatre and the 120-seat Small Theatre. There is free public parking on campus and the E, F, and Z trains (Jamaica Center Subway Station) are within walking distance. The following buses stop at or near the campus: 4, 5, 6, 8, 9, 9A, 17, 24, 30, 31, 41, 42, 44, 54, 56, 60, 65, 77, 83, 84, 85, 110, 111, 112, 113.

Queens Theatre-in-the-Park, Flushing Meadow Park: (718) 760-0064. Housed in a former theater constructed for the 1964 World's Fair, the building was renovated in the mid-1990's. Its circular design allows for a 500-seat main theater and a smaller theater of 100 seats. Plays and performances by noted personalities from the world of music and entertainment are given each season. Ticket prices are reasonable and parking is available.

FISHING

Shell Bank Basin, 158th Street and Cross Bay Boulevard: At least one party boat for saltwater fishing is usually available. This location is 15 to 30 minutes away by car from most areas of Queens.

Sheepshead Bay and City Island: neither site is in Queens. Sheepshead Bay, along Emmons Avenue in Brooklyn, is New York City's major recreational fishing port, with over a dozen large party boats available for fishing in either the Atlantic Ocean or the ocean facing bays of southern Long Island. City Island, in the northeast part of the Bronx, is on Long Island Sound. There usually are at least three large party boats available for fishing on the Sound. Depending where you live in Queens, either site is from 25 to 40 minutes away by car. Departure times of the boats, and their telephone numbers, are listed in newspapers, usually in Friday editions.

GARDENING

Queens Botanical Gardens, 43-50 Main Street in Flushing: (718) 886-3800. Centrally located in Queens across from the eastern side of Flushing Meadow Corona Park, it is easily accessible by car from the Long Island or Van Wyck Expressways or the Grand Central Parkway. The Botanical Gardens cover 39 acres, 18 of which are formal gardens; the remainder is planted with trees and shrubs and is laced with paths. Courses, workshops, and exhibits are available throughout the year. The gardens are open year-round. There is a parking lot.

GOLF COURSES

Clearview, 202-12 Willets Point Boulevard: (718) 229-2570. The course is near the Clearview Expressway and the neighborhoods of Bayside and Whitestone. An 18-hole, par 70 course of 6,263 yards, has small, difficult greens and fairways that are lined with trees. Open all year.

Douglaston, 63-20 Marathon Parkway and Commonwealth Avenue: (718) 428-1617. Near the Grand Central Parkway and the Long Island Expressway and near the neighborhoods of Douglaston and Little Neck, this 18-hole, par 67 course is 5,100 yards. The course is hilly and modestly challenging. Open all year.

Forest Park, Forest Park West Drive and 80th Street: (718) 296-0999. Near the Jackie Robinson Parkway and near the neighborhoods of Forest Hills, Richmond Hill, and Glendale, this 18-hole, par 67 course is 5,820 yards. It has both tight and wide fairways and is hilly in parts.

Kissena, 164-15 Booth Memorial Avenue and 164th Street: (718) 939-4594. Near the Long Island Expressway and near the neighborhood of Flushing. It has an 18-hole, par 64 course of 4,727 yards. There are challenging holes on this smallest of the city's 13 municipal golf courses.

Alley Pond Golf Driving Range, Northern Boulevard and 231st Street: (718) 225-9187. Near the neighborhoods of Douglaston and Bayside. This facility is rented to a concessionaire. The range features approximately 75 tees, about one-half of them are in heated stalls. Open year-round, usually from dawn into the night.

Pitch and Putt Golf Course, Flushing Meadow Park: (718) 271-8182. The course is located near the National Tennis Center and is open year-round, weather permitting.

HORSE RACING

Aqueduct Racetrack, Rockaway Boulevard and 108th Street, South Ozone Park: (718) 641-4700. Located in southern Queens near the Belt Parkway, Van Wyck Expressway, and Cross Bay Boulevard, "The Big A," as Aqueduct is known, is easily accessible by car and also by A line subway, Aqueduct Racetrack station. The thoroughbred racing season is from November to May; gates open at 11:00 a.m. More than 80,000 people can be accommodated. There is a large restaurant and many fast food vendors.

Belmont Park Racetrack: (718) 641-4700 or (516) 488-6000. Technically not in Queens, but in Elmont, Long Island, much of Belmont Park borders the Queens County line. Belmont Park is one of the most famous and attractive racetracks in the country and is the home of the Belmont Stakes, which is run in May, one of horse racing's three most prestigious races. Easily accessible by car from the Cross Island Expressway, Belmont Park Exit. Open for racing from May through July and again in the fall, from September through October. There are a restaurant, clubhouse, and picnic areas. Gates open at 11:00 a.m.

HORSEBACK RIDING

Dixie Dew, 88-11 70th Road: (718) 263-3500, and **Lynne's Riding School, Inc., 88-03 70th Road:** (718) 261-7679. These two private riding academies are located on the northeast periphery of Forest Park, just north of Union Turnpike. The park's dense forest and glaciated topography provide an excellent environment for riders using the many bridle paths that wind for miles through the park (see Forest Park under the heading PARKS).

ICE SKATING

New York City Building in Flushing Meadow Park: (718) 271-1996. The building contains an 18,000 square foot indoor rink. The building, located near the Unisphere, is easily accessible from the Grand Central Parkway, National Tennis Center or Shea Stadium exits.

Ponds: Many ponds in parks in eastern Queens are available for ice skating when the weather permits. Four of the most popular sites are: Bowne Park, 29th Avenue and 155th Street; Captain Tilly Park, Highland Avenue and 165th Street; Crocheron Park, Cross Island Parkway and 33rd Avenue; and Kissena Park, Oak Avenue and 164th Street.

MUSEUMS

American Museum of the Moving Image, 35th Avenue at 36th Street, Astoria: (718) 784-0077; (718) 784-4777 (travel information). Opened in 1988, the museum is devoted to motion pictures, television, video, and digital media. This is a fun place to visit with many interactive exhibits (you can dub your voice into the mouths of famous actors, edit scenes and change soundtracks of movies, make your own flip-card movie, try your hand at animation, and much more). Knowledgeable staff members demonstrate various technologies. There are free movie screenings several times a day. If you get hungry, there are several good Greek restaurants nearby.

Chung-Cheng Art Gallery at St. John's University, Sun Yat Sen Hall, 8000 Utopia Parkway, Jamaica: (718) 990-1526. Housed in the Center for Asian Studies, the gallery is the home of 1,000 Oriental art objects, including Chinese porcelain, paintings, calligraphy, ivory carvings, and jade. The collection spans 13 centuries and also includes photography, pottery, non-Chinese porcelain, stamps, sculpture, Japanese paintings, and Malaysian batik paintings. Approximately 200 art objects are exhibited at a time. Open 9-4, Monday through Thursday, and 12-4 on Friday and Saturday. Closed Sunday. Admission is free. Enter the campus off Union Turnpike and proceed through gate 3 to lot A.

Flushing Town Hall, 137-35 Northern Boulevard at Linden Place, Flushing: (718) 463-770. This Romanesque Revival building was built in 1864 and served as the town hall of the City of Flushing until it became part of New York City in 1898. It houses several small exhibits and serves as a performance space for jazz and other musical entertainment. Good Korean and Chinese restaurants are nearby.

Isamu Noguchi Garden Museum, 32-37 Vernon Boulevard, Long Island City: (718) 721-1932. Sculptor Isamu Noguchi moved his studio from Manhattan to this site in Queens in the 1960's. Besides the sculptures, there is an amazing variety of lamps, many versions of which were inexpensively reproduced in the 1960's and became very popular. The small Japanese garden is lovely. Open April through October, Wednesday through Sunday. Socrates Sculpture Park is nearby. Good Greek restaurants are located on Broadway in the vicinity of 31st Street and further east.

New York Hall of Science, 47-01 111th Street, Flushing Meadow Park: (718) 669-0005. The hall is a hands-on, interactive museum for scientists of all ages. The exhibits not only teach, they are also fun. The Hall of Science was built for the 1964 World's Fair; it was extensively modernized in 1986. A $55 million expansion to double the space of this increasingly popular museum is scheduled to be completed in 2004. There are usually four or five exhibits occurring at the same time. Ongoing exhibits deal with computers, astronomy, biology, sound, light, and color perception. There are also rockets used in the

Mercury and Gemini space programs, as well as a new, large science playground.

P.S. 1 Contemporary Art Center, Jackson Avenue at 46th Avenue, Long Island City: (718) 784-2084. Built as a public school in 1892, this Romanesque Revival building was renovated in 1976 as studio space for artists and as a museum to display contemporary art. A wide range of artistic mediums is presented and artists from all over the world are represented. P.S. 1 has been cited in newspapers in Europe, Russia, and Japan. A major renovation in 1997 enhanced the interior gallery spaces, provided a 19,000-square-foot outdoor exhibit space, and created a small coffeehouse that's handy for a snack. In 1999, P.S. 1 entered into an association with the Museum of Modern Art (MoMA). The nearby Court Square Diner has decent diner food, delicious pastries, and a fantastic custard flan. Greek Astoria and its restaurants are a few minutes away by car.

Queens County Farm Museum, 73-50 Little Neck Parkway, Floral Park: (718) 347-3276. The only farm in Queens sits on 47 acres of what is now Creedmore State Hospital. Seven acres of the site have been landmarked by the City and federal governments and turned into a park run by the city's parks department. The farm had been privately operated from 1772 to 1926. It was purchased by New York State in 1927 and used to provide fresh produce for adjacent Creedmore Psychiatric Hospital, as well as therapy for its patients. In 1973 the city obtained the 7 acres that contained the farmyard and historic buildings. The farmhouse, part of which dates from 1772, was restored in 1985. Besides the farmhouse and outbuildings, there is a two-acre orchard, cow shed, beehives, chicken coop, duck pond, sheep pasture, and cow barn. The museum is open Saturdays and Sundays, 12 to 5 year-round and on Thursdays, 12 to 5, May through September.

Queens Museum of Art, New York City Building, Flushing Meadow Park: (718) 592-9700. It contains the impressive Panorama of the City of New York, a scale-model of the entire city, encompassing over 800,000 buildings, all streets, major infrastructure, and an airplane circling overhead. Various, usually interesting, exhibits are displayed in the museum's several small galleries.

Socrates Sculpture Park, Broadway at Vernon Boulevard, Long Island City: (718) 956-1819. A four-and-a-half-acre site along the East River, it contains large, modern sculptures and has wonderful views of the Upper East Side and northern Roosevelt Island. Open daily year-round. The Isamu Noguchi Garden Museum is nearby. Good Greek restaurants are located on Broadway in the vicinity of 31st Avenue and farther east.

PARKS

Queens has 1.5 million of the city's 2.6 million street and park trees. It also has 7,017 acres of parkland, the largest amount of park space of any of the city's five boroughs. Five large regional parks that range in size from 325 to 1,257 acres serve many of the borough's communities. These parks provide a multitude of activities as well as that rarest of commodities—open space. Three of them—Alley Pond, Cunningham, and Forest Parks—are a nature lover's delight: they contain forests with old trees, ponds left over from the Ice Age, mini-ecosystems, and interesting birds. A description of each of the five parks follows.

Alley Pond Park, Grand Central Parkway, Union Turnpike and Winchester Avenue: (718) 520-5386. This 623-acre park features bicycling, bird-watching, an environmental center, a golf-driving range, 1.5 miles of nature trails, picnic areas, a dozen ballfields, a soccer field, and a tennis center with 16 courts, six of which are covered by a bubble in the winter. It is the natural features of the park, however, that make it special.

Alley Pond Park preserves a landscape that existed in the city before development: estuaries, tidal creeks, spring-fed streams, ponds, marshes, and forests. While development surrounds the park and several highways pass through it, large stretches remain unspoiled. The park has several distinct sections. North of Northern Boulevard is the open water and pebbly beach area of Little Neck Bay, home to many varieties of water fowl and popular with cyclists. South of Northern Boulevard are the wetlands which incorporate an environmental center, Alley Creek, spring-fed freshwater ponds, mudflats, salt marshes, wading birds, and huge fields of phragmites and cattails which are home to pheasants and muskrats. The Oakland Lake area south of Northern Boulevard and west of 223rd Street and Cloverdale Boulevard features a beautiful lake that was formed during the Ice Age. It is ringed by many willow trees and populated by ducks, geese and swans. The area between the Long Island Expressway and Grand Central Parway, known as the Upper Alley, is an area of approximately 200 acres of forest crisscrossed by trails. The area contains five seasonal ponds, each the host to a different type of plant, as well as many wildflowers, birds, salamanders, turtles, and frogs. North of the Upper Alley is The Oaks—a small forest of oak and beech trees and Long Island's largest tulip tree, which is 155 feet tall, 250 years old, and five feet in diameter.

Cunningham Park, Long Island Expressway to Grand Central Parkway, 193rd to 210th Streets: (718) 520-5319. This 350-acre park features: large, open, grass fields, a cross country ski course, bicycling, two miles of nature trails, picnic areas, ballfields, soccer fields, and a tennis center with 20 all-weather courts, 10 of which are covered with a bubble in the winter for indoor play.

The southern portion of the park below Union Turnpike contains 60 acres of forest laced with trails. The moisture-retentive clay soil has spurred the growth of fields of ferns—some 18 varieties have been identified—wildflowers, and many large trees, especially oaks, tulips, and sweet gums. Inside the forest are several diminutive kettle ponds which attract small wildlife, including birds such as herons. The entrance to the forest is by a pathway off Francis Lewis Boulevard.

Flushing Meadows Corona Park, Grand Central Parkway, Flushing Bay, Van Wyck Expressway, 111th to 134th Streets: (718) 507-3000. Known as Flushing Meadow Park, it is the largest park in Queens, 1,255 acres (50 percent larger than Central Park) and the site of both the 1939 and 1964 World's Fairs. It features: two lakes; a marina; the Queens Wildlife Center and Aviary; the New York Hall of Science; the Queens Museum and the Panorama of the City of New York; an indoor ice-skating rink; and the Queens Theatre-in-the-Park. The park also offers bird watching, bicycle paths, a model plane flying field, picnic areas, nine baseball diamonds, seven soccer fields, one cricket field, four handball courts, and five playgrounds, including one for disabled children. The National Tennis Center, which includes Arthur Ashe Stadium and Louis Armstrong stadium, is located at the northern end of the park. The Tennis Center has nine indoor and 27 outdoor courts. Shea Stadium, home of the New York Mets baseball team, is located just north of the Tennis Center.

Flushing Meadow Park was, until the 1930's, the dumping ground for much of the city's coal ashes. Under an inspired plan put into action by Robert Moses, the foremost city planner of his time, the former dump was transformed into the site of the 1939-1940 New York World's Fair. The dump was covered over, the marshland filled in, and a plan developed for the future growth of the park after the fair ended. Two man-made lakes were created south of the nearby Flushing River. They are the 84-acre Meadow Lake, upon which scores of people learn how to sail each year, and the smaller, Willow Lake, left as a wildlife habitat, which takes its name from the willow trees that surround it. The 1939 Fair also left as a legacy the building that houses the current ice-skating rink and the Queens Museum of Art, while the 1964 World's Fair left us the current marina on Flushing Bay at the north edge of the park, a carousel, the Hall of Science, the building that houses the Theatre-in-the-Park, a restaurant that sits elevated above the park—Terrace in the Park—and the Unisphere—a 380 ton, stainless steel globe of the world, about 100 feet tall, and surrounded by fountains. The major park attractions are:

Queens Wildlife Center: (718) 271-1500. This intelligently planned display of North American wildlife was opened to the public in 1996. Rather than compete with larger wildlife centers, the architects created a naturalistic environment for each of the animals which also allows the visitor to stand almost in their world. Featured are: bears, elk, pumas, bobcats, coyotes, bison, prairie dogs, sea lions, eagles, and a host of birds. There is an impressive aviary—and domestic barnyard animals, the latter can be petted and fed by the public.

The New York Hall of Science (see the listing under Museums).

The Queens Museum of Art and the Panorama of the City of New York (see the listing under Museums).

Shea Stadium (see the listing under Baseball Stadium).

Theatre-in-the-Park (see the listing under College and Cultural Offerings).

Forest Park, Myrtle Avenue, Union Turnpike, Park Lane, Park Lane South, and Cypress Hills Cemetery: (718) 520-5900 or 235-4100. The park is 538 acres and features:

an 18-hole golf course, 3.75 miles of nature trails, bridle paths for horseback riding, two riding academies with stables (adjacent to the park), a historic carousel, a bandshell with free band concerts in the summer, 14 tennis courts, athletic fields, and park roads with bicycling and roller blading allowed on summer weekends.

Forest Park is a wonderful natural area, preserved by the foresight of the City of Brooklyn—which bought it for parkland in 1895 (before developers did)—three years before Brooklyn and Queens became part of New York City. The park contains over 400 acres of forest—some of the trees are 150 years old—and is the last densely forested area of mature oak trees in New York City. The oaks—red, white, and scarlet—are often 90 feet tall with three-foot diameters. Among other species in the park are: tulip poplars, known for their unusual flowers, height, and straight growth; pignut hickory, whose nuts, bark, and leaves provide food for animals; sassafras, with its three different shaped leaves and smell of root beer when its leaves are crushed; maples; black birch; and black cherry. The park is also a wonderful geological site. Its topography is a result of the last glacier to affect the Northeast. The park is filled with knobs—hills where the glacier deposited rocks, sand, clay, and other debris, and kettles—depressions formed when huge blocks of ice broke off, depressed the soil for as much as 40 feet and melted forming mini-lakes. While most of the kettles still are water retentive, they have filled in with leaves and other vegetative matter over the centuries. Three nature trails, ranging from one-half to one-and-one-half miles, meander through the forest and past the main natural attractions. Approximately three dozen varieties of birds live in the park, but more than 100 migrating species that use the Atlantic Flyway stop in the park during the spring.

Kissena Park, Oak Avenue, Rose Avenue, Booth Memorial Avenue, Kissena Boulevard, Fresh Meadow Lane: (718) 520-5359. This 234-acre park features: a cross-country ski course, bicycle paths, an environmental center, large pond for fishing and model boating, ice skating, a half-mile nature trail, picnic areas, eight baseball fields, soccer and cricket fields, and 12 tennis courts.

Kissena Park slopes gently from its tree-lined perimeter on Rose Avenue towards Kissena Pond. The pond is used by model boat sailors and by young fishermen trying to hook a carp or sunfish. The eastern half of the park, between 164th Street and Meadow Lane, is a par 64 golf course with some steep slopes ideal for sledding. Kissena Park West, 92 acres, is mainly undeveloped and the home of ring-neck pheasants and rabbits who live among the tall grass. The bicycle path is part of the Greenway bicycle-path system.

OTHER INTERESTING PARKS

Astoria Park, Astoria Park South, 21st St., Hoyt Ave., Ditmars Blvd., East River: (718) 626-8622. This 61-acre park, facing the East River and the East Side of Manhattan, offers impressive views of the Manhattan skyline, Ward Island, and Randall Island, and close-up views of river activity. Soaring above the park are the Triborough Bridge and the Hellgate Railroad Bridge. The park contains 14 tennis courts, play areas, and an Olympic-size swimming pool that was used by athletes to train for the 1936 Olympics.

Francis Lewis Park, Third Avenue, 147th Street, East River, and Parsons Boulevard: (718) 520-5359. A lovely, grassy, 16-acre passive park at the foot of the Whitestone Bridge, it looks out upon the waters of Long Island Sound. A splendid place for a picnic lunch or to get away from it all for an hour or two.

Gantry Plaza State Park, 49th Avenue and the East River: (718) 786-6385. A different kind of park, completed in 1999, it has four brand-new piers (one reserved for fishermen) which jut into the East River and provide magnificent, unobstructed views of the United Nations and the Manhattan skyline. The 2.5-acre park preserves two, towering gantries—huge steel structures, representing 1925 technology—that were used in moving railroad freight cars to and from float barges, which carried the freight cars across New York harbor. The southern end of the park is planted in native grasses and hardy flowers, and contains a children's playground and spray fountain.

McNeil Park, Poppenhusen Avenue, College Place, 115th Street, the East River: (718) 520-5359. Site of a mid-19th Century college building that, in 1937, became the summer City Hall of former Mayor LaGuardia. The building was demolished in 1941, and the site turned into a park. The 28-acre park, located on Long Island Sound at the northern tip of the College Point neighborhood, is a pleasant place to picnic and relax. Besides the blue-gray charm of the sparkling waters on a sunny day, you can watch planes over the Sound silently glide in for a landing at LaGuardia Airport. The surrounding neighborhood is worth exploring; it sports some of the ambience of an old New England town complete with quaint old houses and a white clapboard church.

Udall's Cove Park, Little Neck Parkway and 255th Street: (718) 699-4204. This relatively recent 30-acre addition to the park system provides visitors with views of a functioning tidal inlet ecosystem complete with salt marshes, marsh grasses, mudflats, small fish seeking shelter, and water birds. The park has been left in a natural state.

TENNIS CENTERS

United States Tennis Association National Tennis Center: (718) 760-6200. Located in Flushing Meadow Park, the center is easily accessible by car because it is near the intersection of several major highways: the Grand Central Parkway, the Van Wyck Expressway, and the Long Island Expressway. Parking is free. It is also easily accessible by the Number 7 train, Willets Point station. The tennis center hosts the United States Open Tennis Championship, one of the four major worldwide tennis events. There are two tennis stadiums, nine indoor, year-round courts, and 27 outdoor courts, all of which are lighted for evening play. The facilities are new and attractive, having undergone extensive construction between 1996 and 2000. Nearby neighborhoods are Forest Hills, Flushing, and Jackson Heights.

West Side Tennis Club: (718) 268-2300. The club is located at One Tennis Place, between Burns and Dartmouth Streets in Forest Hills Gardens. It is a private club with 40 tennis courts, a clubhouse, an Olympic-size swimming pool, and restaurant. As the former home of the U.S. Open (the Open outgrew the club's relatively small stadium), the Club offers clay, grass, decoturf, and hartru tennis courts in stately surroundings of green lawns and Tudor-style buildings.

WHERE TO LIVE

Addisleigh Park

(Linden Boulevard to 112th Avenue & 175th Place to 180th Street)

Impressive. That's how to describe the 12 blocks of private homes on quiet, tree-lined streets that are situated just north of the former U. S. Naval Hospital in St. Albans. What's impressive is the quality of the houses, the large lots, the mature trees, the generous use of foundation plantings, the area's human scale (nothing can be seen over three stories high, except for trees), and the exceedingly well maintained appearance of the community.

The houses are a mix of types and styles including wood, brick, Dutch Colonial, and Spanish Revival. Murdock Avenue, a wide street lined with homes that look as if they were owned by doctors, acts as the community's spine, with individual streets radiating at right angles like ribs. Whatever traffic comes into the community, and there isn't much, is funneled down Murdock and kept off the dozen or so streets that are perpendicular to it. The result is a high degree of peace and quiet. Also aiding the area to maintain its identity and tranquility is the Long Island Rail Road: its right-of-way on the eastern flank of Addisleigh Park acts as a barrier to vehicular traffic.

A 10-acre public park and recreation site is located adjacent to the Addisleigh Park community, on its western side. Baisley Pond Park and its 109 acres of water, willow trees, and grassy landscaped areas, ideal for picnicking, is located about a mile southwest of the Addisleigh community. Belmont Racetrack and the 324-acre Cunningham Park with its tennis complex are less than 15 minutes away by car. Shopping is to be found on nearby Linden Boulevard.

To get to Manhattan, the Long Island Rail Road provides a quick ride. From the St. Albans Station it is only 32 minutes to Penn Station. An express bus to Manhattan is also available on nearby Linden Boulevard.

Real Estate

The market value of houses in this area of nicely designed homes ranges from $175,000 to $225,000.

Transportation

HIGHWAYS: Addisleigh Park is about 10 minutes distant from four major highways: the Van Wyck Expressway, the Cross Island Parkway, the Belt/Southern State Parkway, and the Grand Central Parkway. Because these highways interconnect with one another, as well as with other expressways, no part of Queens is much more than 30 minutes away. Manhattan can be reached in about 30 minutes. Kennedy Airport is less than 20 minutes away, LaGuardia Airport is a bit further. It takes only about 10 minutes to get to Nassau County.

SUBWAYS: It takes about five minutes to walk to Linden Boulevard in order to catch the Q4 or Q42 bus for the 10-minute ride to the Jamaica Center-Parsons/Archer terminal of the E, J, and Z trains. Since the trains originate at this stop, there is a good chance to get a seat for your ride to Manhattan. From Jamaica Center Station to Penn Station takes 35 minutes, to the World Trade Center takes 44 minutes, and to Broadway-Nassau-Fulton Streets takes 46 minutes. Lexington Avenue-53rd Street is only 28 minutes away.

COMMUTER TRAINS: It is about a five-minute walk to the Long Island Rail Road St. Albans Station. From this station you can get to Penn Station in Manhattan, without any change of trains, in 32 minutes. Similarly, the Flatbush Avenue Station in Brooklyn is a direct connection, only 28 minutes away.

EXPRESS BUSES: The X63 express bus stops on Linden Boulevard at Merrick Boulevard, about a five to 10-minute walk away. The bus will take you to 1st Avenue and 23rd Street in Manhattan in about 50 minutes.

Shopping

The immediate needs of this area are served by the low key, but limited, shopping on the two blocks of Linden Boulevard between Newburg Street and Farmers Boulevard. There is a bank, a bakery, beauty parlors, delicatessens, a florist, a laundromat, a pharmacy, a Chinese take-out, and a few modest restaurants. A car is necessary to access a wider variety of stores and restaurants. There are a number of additional shopping areas only minutes away. Less than 10 minutes away by car is the Green Acres Shopping Center, one of the largest shopping centers on Long Island.

Education

ELEMENTARY SCHOOL: PS 36, grades K-6, approximately 500 pupils. Located at

187-01 Foch Boulevard. Its reading scores place it in the top half of all public elementary schools in New York City. The school is operating with fewer students than its designed capacity and has an extremely small enrollment for a New York City school.

INTERMEDIATE SCHOOL: IS192, Linden Intermediate School, grades 6-8, is located at 108-89 204th Street. It has about 1,600 students. Its reading scores place it in the top 60 percent of all public middle schools in New York City.

HIGH SCHOOL: The former Andrew Jackson High School building, located at 207-01 116th Avenue, now houses four magnet schools, each with approximately 500 students. The schools are: Law and Government and Community Service Magnet High School; Humanities and the Arts Magnet High School; Business, Computer Applications and Entrepreneurship Magnet High School; and Mathematics, Science, Research and Technology Magnet High School. To attend, students need to apply.

Recreation

Alley Pond Park and Cunningham Park are both 15 minutes away by car. For more information see PARKS in the Where to Play in Queens section.

Roy Wilkens Park: Nearby, on 115th Avenue, it covers 53 acres and is a 10-minute walk away. The park has a public indoor swimming pool.

St. Albans Park: Nearby, on Sayres Avenue, this pretty park covers 10 acres. It is less than a 10-minute walk away.

(Also see Libraries, Private Schools, and Parochial Schools in the Appendix.)

Astoria

(28th Street between Ditmars Boulevard and 21st Avenue)

Twenty-eighth Street between 21st Avenue and Ditmars Boulevard is a pleasant residential block in a community of solid homes. The block, which is on a small hill, is an eclectic mixture of two- and three-story houses and row houses that unexpectedly complement each other. The mature trees on either side of the block help to visually connect the block, while the avenues at each end of the street demarcate the transition to the surrounding neighborhood.

A few short blocks away, although you would never suspect it, it is so quiet, are some of the best restaurants this side of Athens. Ditmars Boulevard is a major shopping street with all the usual urban convenience stores as well as a touch of the exotic—Greek bakeries, tavernas, coffee houses, and local night spots. Although Greeks are the largest single ethnic group in the immediate neighborhood, people of many nationalities make their home in this part of Astoria. And why not? The streets are considered safe, with large numbers of people using them day and night. The presence of an active, bustling commercial district "around the corner" has helped to act as a deterrent to crime. While the local shopping is plentiful, varied, and close, first class recreational facilities are a short distance away. It takes only 10 minutes to walk to the magnificent Astoria Park. Sixty-one acres of parkland bordering the East River offer beautiful views of the Upper East Side of Manhattan and the swift flowing waters of the East River at Hell Gate. It is not unusual to see ships on their way to or from Long Island Sound passing by, scarcely a hundred yards from shore. The park is a well maintained, gently rolling landscape that contains a surprise: an enormous public pool, 330′ by 165′, built during the Depression. The pool has both wading and swimming sections. Tryouts were held here for the 1936 Olympics. An elevated subway line, the N, has its terminus only two blocks away. Passengers can get a seat and be at 59th Street and Lexington Avenue (Bloomingdale's) in 16 minutes. Need I say more!

Real Estate

Based on recent sales, the market value of these three-story, two-family row houses, which entertain the eye with their interesting roof styles and facades, is between $260,000 and $300,000.

Transportation

HIGHWAYS: The nearby Grand Central Parkway provides high-speed access to Upper Manhattan via the Triborough Bridge. The Upper East Side can also be reached via local streets and the 59th Street/Queensboro Bridge. Either route takes less than 15 minutes to drive. LaGuardia Airport is 10 minutes away via the Grand Central Parkway. The

Grand Central Parkway also connects to several other modern highways in Queens, allowing you to reach almost any place in Queens in less than 30 minutes.

SUBWAYS: From the nearby Ditmars Boulevard-Astoria station, the N train will take you to Lexington Avenue-59th Street in 16 minutes, Grand Central Station-42nd Street in 23 minutes, 34th Street-Herald Square in 25 minutes, and 14th Street-Union Square in 28 minutes.

EXPRESS BUSES: Two QM-22 buses stop at 21st Avenue and 26th Street. If there are no delays, they will get you to 34th Street and 3rd or 6th Avenues in Manhattan in 13 minutes, and to 3rd Avenue or 6th Avenue and 59th Street in 10 additional minutes.

Shopping

Two short blocks away, Ditmars Boulevard and 31st Avenue cross each other to create one of the best shopping districts in all of New York City. Stores here are generally upscale, vacancies are nearly non-existent, and there are lots of restaurants.

Scores of good stores fulfill local shopping needs. There are many bakeries, several banks, fruit-and-vegetable stores, dry cleaners, beauty parlors, jewelry stores, pharmacies, real estate offices, nail salons, laundromats, liquor stores, travel agents, florists, groceries, barbers, bagel shops, boutiques, pizza parlors, video stores, vision centers, hardware stores, and meat markets. A supermarket is nearby, as well as a fish store, gourmet deli, health food store, and an ice cream shop.

Education

ELEMENTARY SCHOOL: PS 122, grades K-8, 1,100 pupils. Located at 21-21 Ditmars Boulevard. Its reading scores place it in the top 10 percent of all public elementary schools in New York City.

JUNIOR HIGH SCHOOL: JHS 141, Steinway Junior High School, grades 6-8, is located at 37-11 21st Avenue. It has about 1,100 students. Its reading scores place it in the top 30 percent of all public middle schools in New York City.

HIGH SCHOOL: Long Island City High School is located at 14-30 Broadway; this newly built school opened in 1995 and has about 3,300 pupils. The school uses the latest and most advanced technology (computers, internet, CD-Rom, etc.) as a foundation for learning. The school has an athletic field and a swimming pool. Long Island City High School has two magnet programs that are only open to Queens residents: Technology, Humanities and the Arts Program, and Culinary Institute Program.

Recreation

Astoria Park is a 10- to 15-minute walk away. Flushing Meadow Park is 15 minutes away by car. For more information see PARKS in the Where To Play In Queens section.

(Also see Libraries, Private Schools, and Parochial Schools in the Appendix.)

Auburndale

(193rd Street between 45th and 47th Avenues)

The two blocks on 193rd Street between 45th and 47th Avenues are examples of the uban row-house at its best. In the summer, a luxuriant canopy envelopes the street as large maple trees leaf out and visually unite the block. The houses were built in a Tudor style, with rounded turret-entrances, fieldstone and brick facades, and casement windows. Small gardens are located in the front rather than the back of the houses; many are heavily planted and come alive with seasonal bloom. Both blocks slope downward from 45th Avenue toward 47th and Hollis Court Boulevard. Midway between the blocks, where 193rd street is crossed by 46th Avenue, are several planting islands which are cared for by the adjacent homeowners.

Kissena Park is about a mile away. Its 234 acres offer many field activities as well as a small, but charming, lake. The Clearview Golf Course and the 350-acre Cunningham Park, with its large tennis complex, are less than two miles away. There are also several large churches with day schools in the immediate vicinity.

A supermarket, large meat market, and convenience stores are located around the corner at Utopia Parkway and Hollis Court Boulevard. Rapid transit is available at the Auburndale Station of the Long Island Rail Road, about a 10-minute walk. The train will get you to Penn Station in 27 minutes. The number 7 subway in downtown Flushing is a 15-minute bus ride away. The trip to Grand Central Station takes 26 minutes. There are five bus lines closeby, including Nassau county buses to Great Neck and express buses to Manhattan. An excellent network of expressways is only a few minutes away

Downtown Flushing, with its large shopping district and Asian restaurants, is about 15 minutes away by bus. The restaurants offer an opportunity to taste the food of more than half a dozen Asian cuisines and provide a first-rate gastronomic experience.

Real Estate

The market value of these charming brick, two-story Tudor-style row houses is between $250,000 and $300,000.

Transportation

HIGHWAYS: This area is located only five minutes away from both the Clearview and Long Island Expressways. This allows for rapid connections to all the other highways in Queens. Manhattan is, thus, less than 30 minutes away, LaGuardia Airport is about 20 minutes away, Nassau County is about 20 minutes distant, and almost all of Queens can be reached in less than 30 minutes.

SUBWAYS: The closest subway stop is the Main Street Station of the 7 line, a 15-minute ride away on the B26 or B27 bus. From the Main Street Station to Grand Central Station in Manhattan takes 26 minutes.

COMMUTER TRAINS: The Long Island Rail Road Auburndale Station is a 10-minute walk from this area. Once on board the train, it is only 27 minutes to Penn Station in Manhattan.

EXPRESS BUSES: The QM3 stops not far away on Northern Boulevard at 194th Street. From 194th Street to 3rd Avenue and 57th Street in Manhattan takes approximately 50 minutes.

Shopping

There is a small, but useful, concentration of shops nearby at the junction of Utopia Parkway and Hollis Court Boulevard. Almost as close is a larger array of stores and restaurants on nearby Northern Boulevard.

The restaurants on Northern Boulevard have a nice ambiance, but are not inexpensive. Less expensive fare can be found at the North Shore Diner, and at other smaller establishments. The Oasis Cafe, near Francis Lewis Boulevard, serves wonderful pastry and coffee and is a meeting place for people of all ages.

The area provides the usual array of convenience stores: bakeries, banks, beauty parlors, candy/newspaper stores, florists, groceries, liquor stores, pharmacies, pizza parlors, a large video store, and a supermarket. It also has some specialty stores: a large, quality meat center (D'Alessandro's), an excellent tennis and skate store, a Greek food store, and a tropical fish store.

Education

ELEMENTARY SCHOOL: PS 107, grades K-6, about 1,100 pupils. Located at 167-02 45th Avenue. Its reading scores place it in the top 20 percent of all public elementary schools in New York City.

INTERMEDIATE SCHOOL: IS 25, Adrian Block Intermediate School, grades 7-9, is located at 34-65 192nd Street. It has 1,200 students. Its reading scores place it in the top 20 percent of all public middle schools in New York City.

HIGH SCHOOL: Francis Lewis High School is located at 58-20 Utopia Parkway. It has about 3,200 students. Over 90 percent of its students plan to go on to college, a rate well above the average for New York City high schools. Close to one-third of the students receive Regents-endorsed diplomas or take honors courses, a rate twice that of the average city high school. The school has three popular magnet programs that are only open to Queens residents: Math/Science Research Program; University Scholars Program, which prepares gifted students for acceptance into highly competitive colleges; and Jacob K. Javits Law Institute. The Institute accepts only about 5 percent of students who apply.

Recreation

Kissena Park, Cunningham Park, Alley Pond Park, and Flushing Meadow Park are about 10 to 15 minutes away by car. For more information see PARKS in the Where To Play In Queens section.

(Also see Libraries, Private Schools, and Parochial Schools in the Appendix.)

Bayside

(26th Avenue to 35th Avenue & Bell Boulevard to the Cross Island Parkway)

(39th Avenue between 217 and 223rd Streets; 40th Avenue between 215 and 220th Street)

Fine housing on quiet, suburban style streets can be found in Bayside, especially in the area between 26th and 35th Avenues, east of Bell Boulevard, in Bayside. There are tree-lined streets north and west of John Golden Park and Crocheron Park (the former a beautiful 17-acre green open space overlooking Little Neck Bay and the latter a 45-acre active park with fields and courts). The immediate neighborhood is one of green lawns, foundation plantings, and specimen trees. It is no accident that the Clearview Park Golf course is less than a mile away and the Douglaston Park Golf Course is about two miles away. Sail and power boating on Long Island Sound is available at the Little Neck Bay marina, less than a mile away.

Bell Boulevard forms the western edge of the area. It has about every type of convenience store that one needs, as well as restaurants and taverns. Many of the taverns offer music and entertainment in the evening.

This is car country. The nearest subway is at Main Street, a 20-minute bus ride away. The Long Island Rail Road, however, is much closer to this part of Bayside. A long walk or five minutes on the bus brings you to the Bayside Station. The Long Island Railn Road gets you to Penn Station in 25 minutes. The number 7 Flushing line gets you to Grand Central Station in 26 minutes. Since the train begins at Main Street, passengers have a chance to get a seat.

Schools in this part of Queens are good and their students are among the highest achievers in the city. Queensborough Community College is a modern facility less than two miles away. It offers extensive adult education programs which are open to all. The indoor pool and gymnasium are an especially valuable resource for those wishing to keep in trim.

Real Estate

The market value of most of the more interesting looking one-family houses ranges from the high $300,000s to the high $400,000s, but there are some larger homes on well situated plots that are valued at over $700,000. About a mile to the north, in the Bay Terrace area, a large number of apartments are available in postwar cooperative and condominium buildings. Prices vary from $160,000 to $400,000 for one- to three-bedroom apartments (950 to 1,800 sq. ft.), depending upon whether the building has a pool, health club, doorman and view of Long Island Sound.

Transportation

HIGHWAYS: In about five minutes you can be on the Clearview or Long Island Expressway and thus get to almost any place in Queens in under a half-hour, Nassau County in less than 10 minutes, or to Manhattan in about a half-hour. LaGuardia Airport

is about 20 minutes away; J.F. Kennedy Airport is only a few minutes further. The Throgs Neck and Whitestone bridges, which connect into the New England Thruway, are about 10 minutes away.

SUBWAYS: There are no subways nearby. The closest subway is the 7 line at Main Street in Flushing, about 20 minutes away by bus. From the Main Street station to Grand Central-42nd Street takes 26 minutes, and to either Lexington Avenue-53rd Street or to Rockefeller Center takes 33 minutes.

COMMUTER TRAINS: The Long Island Rail Road Bayside Station is a short bus ride, or a car ride of a few minutes, away. From the Bayside Station to Penn Station in Manhattan is only 25 minutes, a convenience for people traveling to the west side of Manhattan.

EXPRESS BUSES: The QM2 bus on 23rd Avenue and Bell Boulevard and the QM3 bus on Northern Boulevard and Bell Boulevard will get you to 3rd Avenue and 57th Street in Manhattan in about 55 minutes. The QM2 operates seven days a week.

Shopping

There are two distinct centers for shopping in this area: the large suburban-style Bay Terrace Shopping Center on Bell Boulevard and 26th Avenue, and an older established shopping district on Bell Boulevard between 34th Road and Northern Boulevard. The shopping center features a host of stores, among them a large supermarket, a Barnes and Noble super bookstore and coffee bar, a Sony movie theater with six screens, restaurants, a health food store, a kosher delicatessen, several banks, national chain clothing stores, a health club, a weight-loss center, and various convenience stores.

The 3/4 mile stretch along Bell Boulevard has many stores suitable to meet everyday needs as well as a four-screen movie theater and several Irish bars featuring live music. The local restaurants offer a variety of cuisines including Japanese, Italian, and Chinese.

Education

ELEMENTARY SCHOOL: PS 41, grades K-5, approximately 400 pupils. Located at 214-43 35th Avenue. Its reading scores place it in the top 2 percent of all public elementary schools in New York City.

JUNIOR HIGH SCHOOL: JHS 158, Curie Junior High School, grades 6-9, is located at 46-35 Oceania Parkway. It has about 1,200 students. Its reading scores place it in the top 10 percent of all public middle schools in New York City.

HIGH SCHOOL: Bayside High School is located at 208th Street and 32nd Avenue. The school has 2,500 students. A higher percentage of students at Bayside High took and passed Regents examinations in math and science than other high schools in New York City. The school has four magnet programs that are only open to Queens residents: Professional Art Program, Academy of Music Instrumental Program, Academy of Music Vocal Program, and Science/Math Academy of Research and Talent Program (SMART Program). Only about 5 percent of students who applied to SMART were accepted.

Recreation

Alley Pond Park, Cunningham Park, Kissena Park, and Flushing Meadow Park are five to 15 minutes away by car. Golden Park and Crocheron Park are within walking distance. Facilities in the pair of parks include picnic areas, 10 tennis courts, baseball diamonds, and parking lots. For more information see PARKS in the Where To Play In Queens section.

(Also see Libraries, Private Schools, and Parochial Schools in the Appendix.)

Bowne Park

(33rd to 35th Avenues & 156th Street to 163rd Street)

The Bowne Park section of Queens features peaceful blocks of solidly built homes bordered by well tended lawns and flowering shrubs. This prosperous and exclusively residential area offers excellent amenities and value.

The 11-acre Bowne Park, which gives the area its name, has mature trees, grassy spaces for sunning, and a large pond where young and old gather to fish, sail model boats, or feed the ducks. South of the park are many fine homes, especially between 33rd and 35th Avenues and 156th and 163rd Streets. Many homes look as if they could qualify for entry into an All-American Home contest. Colors are subdued. Whites and greys predominate, but muted greens and blues, as well as brown brick, also are to be seen. Building materials vary with the style of the house. The Dutch Colonials are clapboard with shingled roofs; the Spanish Revivals are brick or stucco with ceramic tile roofs. Somehow, the various housing types do not to clash with one another; perhaps because the trees and broad green lawns provide unity or because the colors of the different houses seem to respect one another. On-street parking is ample and most of the houses have their own garages.

Shopping is nearby on Northern Boulevard, while a whole panoply of restaurants, department stores, specialty shops, and services is close by, in downtown Flushing, about five minutes away by car or 10 minutes by bus.

Downtown Flushing is an exciting and robust area. It is the home of the largest concentration of people of Asian ancestry in New York City. Forget about Chinatown in Manhattan. Some of the City's newest and best Chinese restaurants are located here, as are several Korean, Malaysian, and Vietnamese eateries. Bakeries and food stores catering to these new groups add additional variety and interest to the street scene.

Manhattan is not too distant. The number 7 subway line in downtown Flushing provides a mostly elevated ride to Grand Central Station in 26 minutes. The Murray Hill Station of the Long Island Rail Road is a 23 minute ride from Penn Station. And an excellent highway network is quickly and easily accessible.

Real Estate

The single-family homes to be found, block after block, in this area offer a wide variety of housing styles. Many houses are on 60x100 foot lots. The market value of the more pleasing looking houses is about $350,000. Many houses are valued at around $300,000, some are valued at around $400,000.

Transportation

HIGHWAYS: Located in the suburban heart of northeastern Queens, the Bowne Park area is within 10 minutes of four major highways: the Clearview Expressway, the Long Island Expressway, the Cross Island Expressway, and the Van Wyck Expressway. Due to this superb highway network, Manhattan is less than 30 minutes away, LaGuardia Airport and Nassau County are about 20 minutes away, and almost any place in Queens is less than 30 minutes distant.

SUBWAYS: The closest subway stop is the 7 line Main Street station in Flushing, a 10-minute ride away on the Q13 or Q28 bus. From the Main Street Station to Grand Central Station takes 26 minutes.

COMMUTER TRAINS: It is about a 10-minute walk to the Long Island Rail Road Murray Hill Station. From the Murray Hill Station to Penn Station in Manhattan takes only 23 minutes.

EXPRESS BUSES: The QM3 stops on Northern Boulevard at 161st Street. The X51 stops on Sanford Avenue at 164th Street. Depending on where you live in this area, it is a five to 10 minute walk to these stops. From these points to 3rd Avenue and 57th or 59th Street in Manhattan is about 45 minutes.

Shopping

Local shopping is plentiful on Northern Boulevard between 162nd and 155th Streets. On the south side of the boulevard is a small shopping center with a bank, supermarket, pharmacy, and about a dozen retail stores. Also on this side of the boulevard is a branch of the Queens Borough Public Library, a bank, lawyer's offices, a large Chinese restaurant, and an upscale cafe. On the north side of the street are several Korean and Japanese restaurants. Also on the north side is a large children's clothing store, a florist, and an assortment of retail stores selling everything from real estate to floor coverings. There is also a McDonalds and an IHOP on 156th Street. There is considerable additional shopping about a mile or so away on Francis Lewis Boulevard

Education

ELEMENTARY SCHOOL: PS 32, grades K-6, about 1,000 pupils. Located at 171-11 35th Avenue. Its reading scores place it in the top 15 percent of all public elementary schools in New York City.

INTERMEDIATE SCHOOL: IS 25, Adrian Block Intermediate School, grades 7-9, is located at 34-65 192nd Street. It has about 1,200 students. Its reading scores place it in the top 20 percent of all public middle schools in New York City.

HIGH SCHOOL: Francis Lewis High School is located at 58-20 Utopia Parkway. It has about 3,200 students. More than 90 percent of its students report they plan to go on to college, a rate well above the average for New York City high schools. Close to one-third of the students receive Regents-endorsed diplomas or take honors courses, a rate twice that of the average city high school. The school has three popular magnet programs that are only open to Queens residents: Math/Science Research Program; University Scholars Program, which prepares gifted students for acceptance into highly competitive colleges; and Jacob K. Javits Law Institute. The first two are screened programs; the school selects those students who best meet selection criteria. The Institute accepts about 5 percent of students who apply.

Recreation

Flushing Meadow Park, Kissena Park, Cunningham Park, Alley Pond Park are 10 to 15 minutes away by car. For more information see PARKS in the Where To Play Section.

Bowne Park: This beautiful 11-acre park is a five- to 10-minute walk away. It has many old trees and a small lake for model boat sailing and ice-skating.

(Also see Libraries, Private Schools, and Parochial Schools in the Appendix.)

Briarwood

(Hoover & Coolidge Avenues between 138th and 141st Streets)

Then is something special about Hoover Avenue—a street that goes up a hill, curves a bit and then, seemingly, disappears. Undoubtedly, it's the topography that makes this block unique. To walk on the sloping sidewalk, past a row of detached homes, each with its foundation a bit higher than its neighbor's is to make contact with a remnant of the terminal moraine deposited in Queens during the last Ice Age, 10,000 years ago. Oak trees, rustic front yards, wood construction of many of the homes, and exposed earth outcroppings on the street's north side all contribute to maintain the sense of being in a primeval forest. Given the sense of solitude and separateness that pervades the street, it's hard to believe that a major highway and a large shopping center are just a short distance away.

Around the corner from Hoover Avenue is Coolidge Avenue—a two-block-long stretch between 38th and Main Streets, featuring comfortable single-family homes. The houses are post-war, middle class, and sensible. The streets are clean, quiet, and well planted with trees. The street has a gentle aspect engendered by the more than normal setback of the homes from the property line.

Transportation is nearby and convenient. It is about a 10-minute walk to subway and bus lines. The subway gets you to Lexington Avenue in Manhattan in 22 minutes. Manhattan-bound express buses operate on nearby Queens Boulevard. Access to a modern, high-speed expressway system is easily reached. Three major expressways meet not faraway, so travel can be quick and convenient no matter in what direction you're heading. If you travel by air frequently, you'll appreciate the fact that, without being in the flight path, both LaGuardia and Kennedy airports are only 10 minutes away.

On-street parking and garage space is available. Shopping is only a few minutes away by car.

Real Estate

The market value of these two-story, detached, brick-and-wood, one-family homes, many dating from the 1940's, ranges from $250,000 to $275,000 on Hoover Avenue, and from $325,000 to $400,000 on Coolidge Avenue.

Transportation

HIGHWAYS: This is an ideal location from which to get to anyplace quickly. Only a few minutes away from this area, three major highways cross—the Grand Central Parkway, the Van Wyck Expressway, and the Jackie Robinson (Interborough) Parkway—allowing you to connect to other major highways. All the major entry points into Manhattan are little more than 25 minutes away. Nassau County, LaGuardia Airport, and JFK Airport are all about 15 minutes, or less, away.

SUBWAYS: Depending on exactly where one lives, it can be as much as a 15-minute walk to the Union Turnpike station located on Queens Boulevard. The station is amazingly close, however, to Manhattan. Both the E and F express trains stop at Union Turnpike. You can be at Lexington Avenue-53rd Street in 22 minutes (and with only five stops), at Rockefeller Center in 27 minutes, at Grand Central-42nd Street in 35 minutes, and Chambers Street-World Trade Center in 38 minutes. To relieve congestion on the heavily used E and F lines, a new subway connection to Manhattan is under construction and scheduled to open in the year 2002.

COMMUTER TRAINS: The Long Island Rail Road Kew Gardens station is within 10 minutes walking distance of most of the homes in this area. From Kew Gardens Station to Penn Station in Manhattan takes only 17 minutes.

EXPRESS BUSES: The QM18 stops on Lefferts Boulevard and Metropolitan Avenue, Lefferts Boulevard and Austin Street, and Queens Boulevard at Hoover Street. From these stops, it takes 35 to 40 minutes to get to 3rd Avenue and 34th Street and 55 to 60 minutes to get to 3rd Avenue and 57th Street. The QM1 and QM1A buses stop on Union Turnpike and Main Street and are scheduled to get you to 3rd Avenue and 57th Street in 50 minutes. Better yet, both buses operate seven days a week.

Shopping

Most of the local shopping in this area is found on the north side of Queens Boulevard, between Main Street and 87th Avenue and on a few of the side streets. There are three local restaurants—Gateway of India, the Flagship Diner, and Yossi's (Israeli)—as well as several Chinese take-out restaurants. There are also two supermarkets, several pizza parlors, deli/groceries and gourmet delicatessens, banks, dry cleaners, beauty parlors, a bagel store, a hardware store, laundromats, meat markets, and an ice cream shop. Less than a mile away, on Queens Boulevard, on Union Turnpike, and on Main Street, are scores of additional stores and many restaurants.

Education

ELEMENTARY SCHOOL: PS 117, grades K-6, about 1,300 pupils. Located at 85-15 143rd Street. Its reading scores place it in the top 25 percent of all public elementary schools in New York City.

JUNIOR HIGH SCHOOL: JHS 217, R.A. Van Wyck Junior High School, grades 7-8, is located at 85-05 144th Street. It has about 1,200 pupils. Its reading scores place it in the top 55 percent of all public middle schools in New York City.

HIGH SCHOOL: Hillcrest High School is located at 160-05 Highland Avenue. The school was built in 1971 and has about 3,300 students. Overall, the school is academically average. However, the overall figure hides the fact that the school offers magnet Pre-Med, Theatre Arts, and Health Career programs that attract a core group of over 600 gifted students. Students must meet certain criteria to be selected for the Pre-Med Program.

Recreation

Forest Park and Flushing Meadow Park are less than 10 minutes away by car. For more information see PARKS in the Where To Play in Queens section.

Local Park: Within a few minutes walk is a 5.2 acre park on 84th Road.

(Also see Libraries, Private Schools., and Parochial Schools in the Appendix.)

College Point

(Beech Court between 12th and 14th Avenues & 120th Street and College Pt. Blvd.)

Beech Court is a special place on a special site. Formerly the estate of a wealthy silk manufacturer, today it is the site of nine homes that have achieved a sense of privacy and open space that is unusual in New York City. Good site planning and interesting architecture have made the difference.

The homes are well removed from the street and set in a semi-circle surrounding a treed and grassy common green. The mix of architectural styles is eclectic. One of the more modern homes is also one of the most distinguished. It is a 1930's Art Moderne style residence that combines smooth white stucco and glass block and features windows that wrap around the corners. Features of the other houses include porches and columns.

Only a few hundred feet away on 14th Avenue, but visually separated, are other architectural gems: the elegant, 1904 Carnegie library and the white clapboard, New England style First Reformed Church and Sunday School, built in 1872.

Beech Court sits off 14th Avenue and is buffered from the street by its large common space. It is accessible by a semi-circular, perimeter road.

Beech Court's location allows easy pedestrian access to the library as well as to the 14th Avenue shopping district with its many convenience stores. And only a 10-minute walk away is magnificent Hermon A. MacNeil Park, a 28-acre piece of green perched atop a hill overlooking Long Island Sound. The present park was the site of a college that was never built, but which gave College Point its name.

College Point, the community in which Beech Court is located, is surrounded by water on three sides and separated from the rest of Queens by the Whitestone Expressway. This semi-isolation has helped College Point retain a distinct sense of community and New England flavor. Within the community are quaint houses, boat building, and commercial activities related to the sea.

Beech Court provides an opportunity to live in one of New York City's urban villages, with the sense of community, safety, and charm that that implies.

Real Estate

Based on the most recent information, the market value of the houses on this pleasant cul-de-sac range in price from $225,000 to $300,000, with one of exceptional architectural merit valued at over $400,000.

Transportation

HIGHWAYS: Sitting at the end of a small peninsula, College Point has minimal through traffic; however, it is by no means isolated from the rest of the borough and city. Only five minutes away is the Whitestone Expressway, a high speed segment of the interconnected highway system in Queens that can get you to Manhattan or Connecticut in about 25 minutes, almost any place in Queens in about 30 minutes, or to LaGuardia Airport or Nassau County in 15 minutes.

SUBWAYS: There are no nearby subways in College Point. The closest subway station is the Main Street station of the 7 line in Flushing. The ride to the station, on the Q20 bus, takes at least 25 minutes. From the Main Street Station to Grand Central Station in Manhattan takes 26 minutes.

Shopping

There are three main shopping districts. Within easy walking distance is the area's original shopping district, College Point Boulevard, between 14th and 20th Avenues. A little more than half a mile away are two small shopping centers with a total of approxi-

mately two dozen stores. About one mile away, on 20th Avenue at 132nd Street, a modern shopping complex consisting of national chain stores and a large supermarket and bakery, has been built with plenty of parking.

Education

ELEMENTARY SCHOOL: PS 129, grades K-6, about 700 pupils. Located at 128-02 7th Avenue. Its reading scores place it in the top 20 percent of all public elementary schools in New York City.

JUNIOR HIGH SCHOOL: JHS 194, W. H. Carr Junior High School, grades 7-9, is located at 154-60 17th Avenue. It has about 900 students. Its reading scores place it in the top 15 percent of all public middle schools in New York City.

HIGH SCHOOL: Flushing High School is located at 35-01 Union Street. It has about 2,200 pupils, a smaller student body than most New York City High Schools. A third of the students have limited proficiency in English and a quarter are recent immigrants, with Hispanics and Koreans the two largest groups. The school has a Law Related magnet program, The Thurgood Marshall Law Academy, only open to Queens residents.

Recreation

Alley Pond Park, Cunningham Park, Kissena Park are 15 minutes away by car. Herman McNeil Park is within walking distance. For more information see PARKS in the Where To Play In Queens section.

(Also see Libraries, Private Schools, and Parochial Schools in the Appendix.)

Douglaston

(Especially north of 40th Street and west of East Drive)

There are few places prettier than Douglas Manor in Douglaston. Surrounded by Long Island Sound on three sides, this peninsular community provides a nearly perfect residential environment. Separated, but not isolated, from the rest of the city (the Long Island Rail Road will get you to Manhattan in 29 minutes), this upper-middle class enclave offers a way of life few would imagine possible within New York City.

To the west, a few hundred feet off shore, scores of sailboats and other vessels sit at their moorings in Little Neck Bay. The calm waters provide local residents with a perfect anchorage and easy access to boating opportunities on the Sound.

To the south is the 623-acre Alley Pond Park with its environmental center, wetlands, and trails. Also to the south is the 104-acre Douglaston Park Golf Course. On the east side of the peninsula is the 30-acre Udalls Cove Park, which was created as a response to the community's insistence on protecting the Bay's wildlife habitat and wetlands. In the summer, it is not unusual to see men and women in waders fishing in the bay.

The residential area is a blend of brick, wood, and stucco homes built since 1906, when the area was first developed. Although the housing styles vary, with Victorian and Neo-Georgian represented, the overall feeling is closer to that of a prosperous eastern seaboard college town, with lots of large trees and open green lawns. Many of the streets offer romantic views of the water as they wind down a small hill towards the shore.

The peaceful, residential character of the area and the calming waters that surround it help to evoke a shared feeling of community among the residents. Whether it is strolling in the park that runs along the water's edge, or belonging to the Douglaston Club, which is housed in an 1835 country house in the center of the community, or participating in theater groups or local clubs, residents of Douglas Manor are proud of their secure and unique community.

Real Estate

The market value of many of the nicer homes in this area range from $550,000 to $700,000. There are some homes, often with six or more bedrooms and on large lots, that can cost over $2 million.

Transportation

HIGHWAYS: Althougth this community is located in eastern Queens, almost on the Nassau County border, it is still possible to get to Manhattan in about a half-hour, during non-rush hours. JFK Airport and LaGuardia Airport are about 25 minutes away. The Throgs Neck and Whitestone bridges are about 15 minutes away. Nassau County and its towns, such as Great Neck and Lake Success, are almost next door, a few minutes away.

SUBWAYS: The nearest subway to this area is the 7 line at Main Street in Flushing, a 20-minute or more bus ride away preceded by a long walk. From Main Street to Grand Central-42nd Street takes 26 minutes. Instead, most people traveling into Manhattan rely upon the Long Island Rail Road.

COMMUTER TRAINS: The Long Island Rail Road has a station in Douglaston. It has parking space for many cars, as well as being easy to walk to. From the Douglaston Station to Penn Station in Manhattan takes, on average, just 29 minutes.

Shopping

Most small shopping needs can be taken care of in the immediate area of Douglaston Parkway and Northern Boulevard. There are a bank, pizza parlor, pharmacy, hardware store, liquor store, shoe-repair store, grocery, gourmet deli, and travel agent. There also are a number of restaurants and up-scale bars located adjacent to the Long Island Rail Road station. An excellent and popular diner, the Seville, is located nearby on Northern Boulevard. Most other shopping needs can be satisfied by a less than five-minute car ride to either Bell Boulevard, to the west, or by heading east to Little Neck Parkway.

Education

ELEMENTARY SCHOOLS: PS 98, grades K-5, about 300 pupils. Located at 40-20 235th Street. Its reading scores place it in the top 2 percent of all public elementary schools in New York City. PS 98 has consistently ranked high; usually nearly 90 percent of its students read at or above grade level.

JUNIOR HIGH SCHOOL: JHS 67, Louis Pasteur Junior High School, grades 6-9, is located at 51-60 Marathon Parkway. It has about 1,200 students. Its reading scores place it in the top 5 percent of all public middle schools in New York City.

HIGH SCHOOL: Benjamin Cardozo High School, located at 5700 223rd Street, has about 4,000 students. It is one of the best academic high schools in New York City. With the exception of the specialized city high schools, such as the Bronx High School of Science, Townsend Harris in Queens, and Stuyvesant in Manhattan, Benjamin Cardozo's students have had the highest SAT scores in citywide tests for several years. Over 90 percent of the students say they plan to go to college after graduation. The school has three magnet programs that are only open to Queens residents: Da Vinci Science-Math Research Institute, Performing Dance Program, and Mentor Law and Humanities Institute. The first two are screened programs; the school selects those students who best meet selection criteria. Only about 5 percent of the approximately 2,000 students who applied to the Research Institute Program were accepted; only 7 percent of the approximately 2,200 students who applied to the Mentor Program were accepted. Benjamin Cardozo is a relatively new school; built in 1967 on the site of a former golf course, it has a large athletic field.

Recreation

Alley Pond Park, Cunningham Park, Kissena Park are 5 to 10 minutes away by car.

Udall's Cove Park is within walking distance. For more information see PARKS in the Where To Play In Queens section.

(Also see Libraries, Private Schools, and Parochial Schools in the Appendix.)

Flushing

(146th Street between 29th Road and Bayside Avenue)

Scarcely a mile from the web of stores, hotels, parking lots, markets, and Asian restaurants that make up the cosmopolitan world of downtown Flushing is a tidbit of urban/suburban living tucked away on what appears to be a private street. Perhaps it is its hidden quality, or the large trees, or the brickwork of the handsome pair of houses at the entrance, or the sense of privacy that a cul-de-sac gives, that work the magic, but whatever it is, it is a small, private, and special place.

Besides the two small stone mansions on either side of 146th Street and Bayside Avenue, there are a small number of 1920's homes on the block, which has been dead ended and turned into a pleasant residential cul-de-sac.

The immediate neighborhood also does not lack charm. There are some eye-catching houses on Bayside Avenue at 145th Street, as well as several between Parsons Boulevard and Union Street and between 33rd and 34th Avenues

Convenience shopping and recreation are also nearby. The 10 acres of Memorial Field of Flushing is about 10 minutes away by foot. Bowne Park, with its large trees and small pond is about 3/4 of a mile away. A supermarket and neighborhood stores are a 10-minute walk away. A 20-minute walk, or a short bus ride, brings you to the Main Street stop of the number 7 IRT subway. A block away is the Flushing Station of the Long Island Rail Road. The number 7 will get you to Grand Central Station in 26 minutes; the LIRR will get you to Pennsylvania Station in 17 minutes. If you wish to go further afield, an excellent highway network is five minutes away and will take you quickly in any direction.

And for those who desire a bit of the exotic, downtown Flushing is relatively close, offering a diverse sampling of Asian culture. Since the 1970's, a part of downtown Flushing has become home to many Asian immigrants. Scores of restaurants, as well as bakeries and food stores, catering to Chinese, Korean, Thai, Malaysian, and other people from Southeast Asia flourish there.

Real Estate

The market value of the dozen or so homes in and around this pleasant cul-de-sac is estimated at between $320,000 and $350,000.

Transportation

HIGHWAYS: In five minutes you can be on the Whitestone Expressway and on your way to Manhattan or Connecticut, each about 25 minutes away. LaGuardia Airport is a mere 10 minutes away, Nassau County is 15 minutes away, and most any part of Queens is within 30 minutes.

SUBWAYS: To reach the closest subway to this area requires a 10-minute bus ride on the Q16 bus to the 7 line Main Street Station in Flushing. From the Main Street Station to Grand Central Station in Manhattan takes 26 minutes.

EXPRESS BUSES: The QM2A stops, not far away, at 146th Street and Willets Point Boulevard. From there to 3rd Avenue and 57th Street in Manhattan takes about 45 minutes.

Shopping

There are two nearby shopping centers that serve this area. Stores located at the junction of Willets Point Boulevard and Parsons Boulevard include a supermarket, two banks, and over a dozen convenience stores with ample parking. Another shopping area, on Union Street, between 28th Avenue and 31st Road, has a branch public library, a bank, and a similar mix of convenience and service stores, including a Korean supermarket. In addition, Downtown Flushing, with its department stores, many retail stores, and scores of southeast Asian restaurants is only a mile away.

Education

ELEMENTARY SCHOOL: PS 21, grades K-6, about 1,100 pupils. Located at 147-36 26th Avenue. Its reading scores place it in the top quarter of all public elementary schools in New York City.

JUNIOR HIGH SCHOOL: JHS 185, E. Bleeker Junior High School, grades 7-9, is located at 147-26 25th Drive. It has about 900 students. Its reading scores place it in the top 20 percent of all public middle schools in New York City.

HIGH SCHOOL: Flushing High School is located at 35-01 Union Street. It has about 2,200 pupils, a smaller student body than most New York City High Schools. A third of the students have limited proficiency in English and a quarter of the students are recent immigrants, with Hispanics and Koreans the two largest groups. The school has a magnet program that is only open to Queens residents: The Thurgood Marshall Law Academy. About 25 percent of the students that applied for this program were accepted.

Recreation

Flushing Meadow Park, Kissena Park, Cunningham Park, and Alley Pond Park are 10 to 15 minutes away by car. For more information on the facilities in these parks see PARKS in the Where To Play In Queens section.

Local Parks: Memorial Field of Flushing is 10.2-acres of athletic fields, only a 10-minute walk away. PS. 214 has a 1.4-acre playground and is only a five-minute walk away.

(Also see Libraries, Private Schools, and Parochial Schools in the Appendix.).

Forest Hills Gardens & Vicinity

(Burns Street to Juno Street/Whitson Street & Union Turnpike to 69th Avenue)

No community in Queens offers as much as Forest Hills Gardens. Long associated with the world famous Forest Hills Tennis Tournament, this once exclusive community contains some of the finest and most expensive homes in Queens. This is proved by the fact that houses and apartments are gobbled up nearly as soon as they come onto the market

Forest Hills Gardens' special appeal is a result of good planning, finely executed romantic architecture, lush landscaping, and an adherence to building standards and an architectural style that have perpetuated the area's charm and character.

In 1909 the Russell Sage Foundation purchased approximately 160 acres of land in Queens to build a community of fine homes, open spaces, and gardens only 15 minutes from the center of Manhattan. They succeeded in creating a model English town, complete with shops, small offices, an elementary school, parks, churches, open spaces, brick streets, restaurants, a commuter railroad station, and a handsome main square, complete with clock tower, that is the focal point around which the community radiates.

The houses are made mainly of brick, stucco, or even concrete. Peaked roofs of tile or slate predominate. The streets are curvilinear, creating a pleasant visual landscape and assuring privacy. There are only two straight through streets in the entire community, and many streets end in cul-de-sacs ringed with one- and two-family homes. The Gardens was extensively landscaped and is heavily planted with many varieties of trees and flowering shrubs. In the spring flowering varieties, such as rhododendron, azalea, wisteria, forsythia, flowering cherry, crabapple, dogwood, and horse chestnut, create a beautiful spectacle.

The Forest Hills Gardens Corporation, an organization of residents, took over the project in the 1920's when it was half finished. The Corporation maintains the streets, which are privately owned, as well as the distinctively styled street lamps, the parks, and public spaces. In the fall, it is responsible for removing the leaves and, in the winter, for removing the snow.

Lexington Avenue and 53rd Street is only four express stops or 17 minutes away by subway; Penn Station is 15 minutes from Forest Hills by the Long Island Rail Road.

Abundant shopping and many restaurants are located immediately adjacent to the Gardens on both Austin Street and Queens Boulevard. Many of the stores and restaurants are upscale.

Real Estate

While houses in Forest Hills Gardens can cost $1 million (or more), there also are houses that have sold recently for $500,000. The size of the house and its location within the Gardens are the key determinants of its cost. Many of the houses are built in a Tudor style; others have tile roofs and stucco walls. Most homes have wood-burning fireplaces. While there are mansions, there also are detached, single-family houses and attached row-houses. Whatever the type of house, the overall effect is pleasing, due to the well planned layout of the Gardens and the lavish landscaping. Based on recent sales, the market value of most single-family houses ranges from $550,000 to $990,000, with the largest number of homes selling for between $600,000 and $700,000. A nearby luxury high-rise coopera-tive apartment building—with doorman, health club, and swimming pool—has studio apartments that sell for about $95,000 to $125,000, with a $425 to $600 monthly mainte-nance charge; one-bedroom apartments sell for $140,000 to $170,000, with a $500 to $750 monthly maintenance charge; two-bedroom apartments sell for $200,000 to $275,000 with a $900 to $1,300 monthly maintenance charge; and three-bedroom apart-ments sell for $350,000 to $425,000 with monthly maintenance charges of $1,100 to $1,600 or more.

Immediately to the south of Forest Hills Gardens, between Harrow Street and Juno Street from Ascan Avenue to 69th Avenue, is the Van Court area; which consists of about a dozen blocks of nice housing that is less expensive than the housing in Forest Hills Gardens.

Transportation

HIGHWAYS: It always seems incredible, but it is possible to get to Manhattan in lit-tle more than 15 minutes. In fact, this is the ideal location for highway trips. Within approximately six minutes of your door are major east-west and north-south highways. LaGuardia Airport is a mere 10 minutes away; JFK is less than 15 minutes away; the Whitestone and Throgs Neck bridges, that connect to the Bronx, Westchester, and Connecticut, are each little more than 15 minutes away. Brooklyn is a mere 10 minutes away. In fact, almost all of Queens is accessible by car in little more than 20 minutes thanks to a superb network of four modern east-west highways and three north-south expressways/parkways; few areas in the metropolitan area are so well connected.

SUBWAYS: The Continental Avenue station is an express stop on the E and F sub-way lines, as well as a stop on the R and G lines. From this station, using the E or F train, Lexington Avenue-53rd Street is only four stops or 17 minutes away. Other destinations, such as 47th-50th Streets-Rockefeller Center can be reached in 21 minutes, Grand Central-42nd Street in 28 minutes, and Chambers Street-World Trade Center in 35 min-utes. To relieve congestion on this busy line, a new subway connection to Manhattan is under construction. It is scheduled to be in service in the year 2002.

COMMUTER TRAINS: The Long island Rail Road provides the quickest ride into Manhattan. From the station in Forest Hills to Penn Station on the west side of Manhattan takes only 15 minutes.

EXPRESS BUSES: The QM11 bus stops on Queens Boulevard at Ascan Avenue. From there to Wall Street takes 50 minutes, barring traffic delays. The X63, X64, and X68 all stop on Queens Boulevard at 78th Avenue. Their destination is 1st Avenue and 21st Street, which is about 40 minutes away. Some X68 buses also go to 3rd Avenue and 51st Street, a convenience for those heading uptown. The QM18 also stops at Queens Boulevard and 78th Avenue. It is scheduled to arrive at 34th Street and 3rd Avenue in 35 minutes and 3rd Avenue and 57th Street in 55 minutes.

Shopping

The area is served by four major shopping streets. In terms of variety and the number of quality stores, there is no better neighborhood shopping in Queens. The area compares well to many of the better neighborhood shopping areas in Manhattan. The four streets are: Austin Street from Ascan Avenue to Yellowstone Boulevard; Continental Avenue from Queens Boulevard to Station Square; Queens Boulevard from Union

Turnpike to Yellowstone Boulevard; and Metropolitan Avenue from Union Turnpike to Yellowstone Boulevard.

There are three, first-run movie theaters—with a total of 16 screens—in the area. Two of these theaters, and a Barnes and Noble super bookstore, are located within a block of Austin Street and Continental Avenue. Good restaurants and cafes abound here. At last count there were at least 10 restaurants and three coffee houses/cafes. Food ranges from Japanese to Southwest USA cuisine. Other restaurants include: Pizzeria Uno; UJ's, a 1950's style upscale diner; Sargent Garcia, Mexican food; Melange, a supper club/restaurant; Piu Bello, a slick, Italian gelateria; and two Starbucks Coffee bars. One block north of Austin Street, a three-quarter-mile strip along Queens Boulevard has approximately 20 restaurants, including Tutta Pasta reviewed in the Zagat Survey of New York Restaurants. There are several other good Italian restaurants, as well as Chinese, Japanese, Thai, and Indian. And there is still more. On nearby Metropolitan Avenue (two minutes by car), along a three-quarter-mile strip, is the top notch Bistro Metro Restaurant (Continental food), Alberto and Tutto Bene (Italian), and Chalet Alpina (German). There is also a brick-oven pizza restaurant (Dee's), a coffee bar, and an old fashioned candy store, featuring home made ice cream and malteds (Eddie's Sweet Shop). The area also has its share of pizza parlors, fast food places, and yogurt/ice cream stores, but they are generally unobtrusive.

With all this food around, it's nice to know that the area has several fitness and weight-loss centers. There also are plenty of banks, beauty parlors, nail salons, vision centers, stock brokers, pharmacies, and dry cleaners, as well as other types of stores: liquor, pet, florist, photo, meat, bagel, bakery, fruit-and-vegetable, grocery, major electronic/appliance, music (including Sam Ash for musical instruments), and several gourmet delicatessens and supermarkets. Austin Street also has Strawberry, Gap, Banana Republic, and Benetton for clothes, and Lechters for housewares. Finally, for those who like antiques, there are about a dozen antique stores on Metropolitan Avenue.

Education

ELEMENTARY SCHOOLS: Two K-6 public schools, PS 101 with about 600 pupils and PS 144 with about 700 pupils, serve this area. PS 101 is located at 2 Russell Place in Forest Hills Gardens. Its reading scores place it near the top 5 percent of all public elementary schools in New York City. PS 144, located at 93-02 69th Avenue, draws students west of 71st/Continental Avenue. Its reading scores place it in the top 10 percent of all public elementary schools in New York City.

JUNIOR HIGH SCHOOL: JHS 190, Russell Sage Junior High School, grades 7-9, is located at 68-17 Austin Street. It has about 1,400 students. Its reading scores place it near the top 15 percent of all public middle schools in New York City.

HIGH SCHOOL: Hillcrest High School is located at 160-05 Highland Avenue . The school was built in 1971 and has about 3,300 students. Overall, the school is academically average in comparison to other high schools in the New York City school system. However, the overall figures hide the fact that the school offers a magnet Pre-Med Program that attracts a core group of over 200 academically gifted students. This program (and the school's Theatre Arts Program, which has over 100 students) is a screened program; the school selects those students who best meet selection criteria. In addition there is a Health Careers Program that attracts about 300 students who are chosen according to the following formula: 16 percent have reading scores above average, 68 percent read within the average range, and 16 percent read below average.

Recreation

Forest Park: some of it can be reached on foot; the rest is accessible by car. Flushing Meadow Park is five minutes away by car. For more information see PARKS in the Where To Play In Queens section.

Austin Street Playground: You can walk to this 1.1 acre playground in 5 to 10 minutes. Features: early-childhood play equipment, basketball for older kids, and benches to watch the action.

(Also see Libraries, Private Schools, and Parochial Schools in the Appendix.)

Forest Hills–
North of Queens Boulevard

(Jewel Avenue to 67th Road & 108th Street to Peartree Avenue/113th Street)

North of Queens Boulevard, between 70th Avenue and 67th Road and 108th Street and the Grand Central Parkway service road, are nearly two dozen blocks of well kept, substantial private homes near good public schools and within walking distance of one of the city's best neighborhood shopping districts.

The homes are gracious, older suburban-type structures, usually two to two-and-a-half stories high of various interesting architectural styles. Ample landscaping, low density, and clean streets enhance the area's attractiveness.

The local public schools are among the best in the City; students attending the neighborhood elementary, junior high, and high school consistently rank high on achievement tests. Forest Hills High School, with its fine reputation and suburban-size athletic field is within 10 minutes of every block in the area.

Excellent and inexpensive higher education is also located at the community's doorstep. The City University of New York's 52-acre Queens College campus is a mile and a half away. And St. John's University is only 10 minutes by car.

Excellent shopping is available on Queens Boulevard, as well as on Continental Avenue, and especially on Austin Street which is home to many trendy clothing stores and fine restaurants. Two movie theatres with a total of 11 screens are located little more than a block from the center of the shopping area.

Recreational facilities are nearby. They include: a modern "Y" with an indoor swimming pool on 108th Street; the West Side Tennis Club in Forest Hills Gardens; and Flushing Meadow Park, site of the 1939 and 1964 World's Fairs. The park's 1,255 acres contain two small lakes, an indoor ice skating rink, a small zoo, an excellent science museum, a running track, and ballfields and bicycle paths, as well as a world class tennis stadium and Shea Stadium, home of the New York Mets baseball team.

Should you desire to go into Manhattan, Lexington Avenue and 53rd Street are only four express stops and 17 minutes away.

Real Estate

Based on recent sales, the market value of the handsome houses available in many architectural styles ranges from $500,000 to $800,000, with many sales occurring around $550,000. On nearby Queens Boulevard, a luxury high-rise cooperative apartment building—with doorman, health club, and swimming pool—has studio apartments that sell for

about $95,000 to $125,000, with a $425 to $600 monthly maintenance charge; one-bedroom apartments sell for $140,000 to $170,000, with a $500 to $750 monthly maintenance charge; two-bedroom apartments sell for $200,000 to $275,000 with a $900 to $1,300 monthly maintenance charge; and three-bedroom apartments sell for $350,000 to $425,000 with monthly maintenance charges of $1,100 to $1,600 or more.

Transportation

HIGHWAYS: It is possible to get to Manhattan in about 15 minutes via the Queens Midtown Tunnel. Actually, there are six ways to get to Manhattan in less than 30 minutes, from the Grand Central Parkway/Triborough Bridge to the Brooklyn-Queens Expressway/Brooklyn Bridge including four other routes in between. If you are heading east, almost the entire borough can be reached in 20 minutes, as well as Nassau County. LaGuardia Airport in less than 10 minutes away; JFK Airport is less than 15 minutes away.

SUBWAYS: The Continental Avenue station is an express stop on the E and F subway lines, as well as a stop on the R and G lines. From this station, using the E or F train, Lexington Avenue-53rd Street is only four stops or 17 minutes away. Other destinations, such as 47th-50th Streets-Rockefeller Center can be reached in 21 minutes, Grand Central-42nd Street in 28 minutes, and Chambers Street-World Trade Center in 35 minutes. To relieve congestion on this busy line, a new subway connection to Manhattan is under construction. It is scheduled to be in service in the year 2002.

COMMUTER TRAINS: It is about a 10-minute walk to the Long Island Rail Road Forest Hills Station. From there, it is only a 15-minute ride to Penn Station in Manhattan.

EXPRESS BUSES: The QM12 stops on Yellowstone Boulevard and 67th, 68th, and 69th Avenues. From these stops to 3rd or 6th Avenues and 59th Street in Manhattan takes 35 minutes barring any traffic delays. The QM4 stops at 69th Road and 112th, 110th, and 108th Streets. Its scheduled running time to 6th Avenue and 36th Street in Manhattan is 35 minutes.

Shopping

The area is served by four major shopping streets. In terms of variety and the number of quality stores, there is no better neighborhood shopping in Queens. The area compares well to many of the better neighborhood shopping areas in Manhattan. The four streets are: Austin Street from Ascan Avenue to Yellowstone Boulevard; Continental Avenue from Queens Boulevard to Station Square; Queens Boulevard from Union Turnpike to Yellowstone Boulevard; and 108th Street from 65th Avenue to 63rd Road.

There are two first-run movie theaters—with a total of 11 screens—in the area. These theaters, and a Barnes and Noble super bookstore, are located within a block of Austin Street and Continental Avenue. Good restaurants and cafes abound here. See the Forest Hills Gardens section on shopping for details. One block north of Austin Street, a three-quarter-mile strip along Queens Boulevard has approximately 20 restaurants. And there is still more: There are six restaurants on 108th Street, including kosher Chinese, Bukharian, and Italian, as well as appetizing stores featuring Russian and Middle Eastern foods.

There also are fitness and weight-loss centers, plenty of banks, beauty parlors, nail salons, vision centers, stock brokers, pizza parlors, pharmacies, and dry cleaners, as well as other types of stores: liquor, pet, florist, photo, meat, bagel, bakery, fruit and vegetable, grocery, major electronic/appliance, music (including Sam Ash), several gourmet delicatessens, and supermarkets. Austin Street also has Strawberry, Gap, Banana Republic, and Benetton for clothes, and Lechters for housewares.

Education

ELEMENTARY SCHOOL: PS 196, grades 1-5, about 600 pupils. Located at 71-35 113th Street. Its reading scores place it in the top one to 3 percent of all public elementary schools in New York City, a position it has held for many years.

JUNIOR HIGH SCHOOL: JHS 157, S. A. Halsey Junior High School, grades 6-9, has about 1,700 pupils and is located at 102nd Street and 64th Avenue. Its reading scores place it near the top 20 percent of all public middle schools in New York City.

HIGH SCHOOL: Forest Hills High School is located at 67-01 110th Street. It has about 3,500 students. Student achievement test results show that students at Forest Hills High School perform better academically than students at the average New York City high school. The school has two magnet programs that are only open to Queens residents: Law and Humanities Institute Program, and the Management and Finance Program. The former program accepts only about 5 percent of the students that apply.

Recreation

Forest Park: You can reach any part of this 538-acre park in less than 10 minutes by car. Flushing Meadow Park is five minutes away by car. For more information about these parks and their facilities see PARKS in the Where To Play In Queens section.

(Also see Libraries, Private Schools, and Parochial Schools in the Appendix.)

Forest Hills–The Closes

(Austin Street to Queens Boulevard & 75th Avenue to 76th Avenue)

The Closes are two blocks of English-style charm and greenery set between two excellent shopping streets in Forest Hills. Yet, so well designed are the Closes, you could live there and never know the outside world existed. These rustic, two-story, Tudor-style row houses form a secure and impenetrable wall. But once on the inside, there is a feeling of coziness accentuated by exposed wood beams, fireplaces, and brick. Behind the houses is a surprise: a large common green space runs the length of each block and provides a pleasant sanctuary for the residents. The common green allows neighbors to get to know one another if they so wish, and it provides children a space to play safely. There is also a small public playground immediately across the street from the Closes.

The Closes were built in the mid-1920's. There are two separate Closes, each built a bit differently. Arbor Close houses have Tudor-style half-timbering, gables, and slate roofs. The houses in Forest Close have bay windows, eaves over the doorways, and dormers. All the houses are built out of brick.

The Closes are adjacent to the upscale Forest Hills Gardens community. There is excellent shopping, as well as first-class dining and entertainment, on Austin Street, Queens Boulevard, and Continental Avenue, The local shopping area was, only a generation ago, referred to as "the village." Today, besides the gourmet food stores, bakery outlets, and contemporary clothing stores, there are two movie theatres with a total of 11 screens. All are within easy walking distance of the Closes. And for those who want to be close to Manhattan, it is only four express stops and 17 minutes away. If you choose to ride the Long Island Rail Road, you can get to Penn Station in only 15 minutes. And if you have a car, the Closes provide garage space. This part of Queens is less than five minutes from an extensive highway network that will take you, at high speed, in any direction.

Real Estate

The fine design of the Olmstead Brothers and Robert Tappen, strong maintenance agreements, and the charming architectural detailing of these row houses have created a unique, safe, and self-contained environment. Based on recent sales, the market value of these houses ranges from $325,000 to $450,000. On nearby Queens Boulevard, a luxury high-rise cooperative apartment building—with doorman, health club, and swimming pool—has studio apartments that sell for about $95,000 to $125,000, with a $425 to $600 monthly maintenance charge; one-bedroom apartments sell for $140,000 to $170,000, with a $500 to $750 monthly maintenance charge; two-bedroom apartments sell for $200,000 to $275,000, with a $900 to $1,300 monthly maintenance charge; and three-bedroom apartments sell for $350,000 to $425,000, with monthly maintenance charges of $1,100 to $1,600 or more.

Transportation

HIGHWAYS: It always seems incredible, but it is possible to get to Manhattan in little more than 15 minutes. In fact, this is the ideal location for highway trips. Within approximately six minutes of your door are major east-west and north-south highways. LaGuardia Airport is a mere 10 minutes away; JFK is less than 15 minutes away; the Whitestone and Throgs Neck bridges, that connect to the Bronx, Westchester, and Connecticut, are each little more than 15 minutes away. Brooklyn is a mere 10 minutes away. In fact, almost all of Queens is accessible by car in little more than 20 minutes, thanks to a superb network of four modern east-west highways and three north-south expressways/parkways; few areas in the metropolitan area are so well connected.

SUBWAYS: The Continental Avenue station is an express stop on the E and F subway lines, as well as a stop on the R and G lines. From this station, using the E or F train, Lexington Avenue-53rd Street is only four stops or 17 minutes away. Other destinations, such as 47th-50th Streets-Rockefeller Center can be reached in 21 minutes, Grand Central-42nd Street in 28 minutes, and Chambers Street-World Trade Center in 35 minutes. To relieve congestion on this busy line, a new subway connection to Manhattan is under construction. It is scheduled to be in service in the year 2002.

COMMUTER TRAINS: The Long island Rail Road provides the quickest ride into Manhattan. From their station in Forest Hills to Penn Station on the west side of Manhattan takes only 15 minutes.

EXPRESS BUSES: The QM11 bus stops on Queens Boulevard at Ascan Avenue. From there to Wall Street takes 50 minutes, barring traffic delays. The X63, X64, and X68 all stop on Queens Boulevard at 78th Avenue. Their destination is 1st Avenue and 21st Street, which is about 40 minutes away. Some X68 buses also go to 3rd Avenue and 51st

Street, a convenience for those heading uptown. The QM18 also stops at Queens Boulevard and 78th Avenue. It is scheduled to arrive at 34th Street and 3rd Avenue in 35 minutes and 3rd Avenue and 57th Street in 55 minutes.

Shopping

The area is served by four major shopping streets. In terms of variety and the number of quality stores, there is no better neighborhood shopping in Queens. The area compares well to many of the better neighborhood shopping areas in Manhattan. The four streets are: Austin Street from Ascan Avenue to Yellowstone Boulevard; Continental Avenue from Queens Boulevard to Station Square; Queens Boulevard from Union Turnpike to Yellowstone Boulevard; and Metropolitan Avenue from Union Turnpike to Yellowstone Boulevard.

For details about these shopping streets see Shopping in the Forest Hills Gardens & Vicinity section.

Education

ELEMENTARY SCHOOL: PS 101, grades K-6, about 600 pupils. Located at 2 Russell Place in Forest Hills Gardens. Its reading scores place it near the top 5 percent of all public elementary schools in New York City.

JUNIOR HIGH SCHOOL: JHS 190, Russell Sage Junior High School, grades 7-9, is located at 68-17 Austin Street. It has about 1,400 students. Its reading scores place it near the top 15 percent of all public middle schools in New York City.

HIGH SCHOOL: Hillcrest High School is located at 160-05 Highland Avenue. The school was built in 1971 and has about 3,300 students. Overall, the school is academically average in comparison to other high schools in the New York City school system. However, the overall figures hide the fact that the school offers a magnet Pre-Med Program that attracts a core group of over 200 academically gifted students. This program (and the school's Theatre Arts Program, which has over 100 students) is a screened program; the school selects those students who best meet selection criteria. In addition there is a Health Careers Program that attracts about 300 students.

Recreation

Forest Park: You can reach any part of this park in 10 minutes by car. Flushing Meadow Park is five minutes away by car. For more information see PARKS in the Where To Play In Queens section.

Austin Street Playground: You can walk to this 1.1-acre playground in a minute. Features: early-childhood play equipment, basketball, and benches to watch the action.

(Also see Libraries, Private Schools, and Parochial Schools in the Appendix.)

Hollis

(Hollis Park Gardens area, 191st Street to 195th Place & 90th Avenue to Hillside Avenue)

Quality is the difference between an ordinary real estate development and one like Hollis Park Gardens. Hollis Park Gardens consists of five blocks of varied, tastefully designed, single-family homes dating from the 1920's, set amongst lots of trees and open space. The development also includes one apartment house which acts as a landmark for the community. One of the blocks has an especially long, grassy median that attracts sunbathers.

Housing types vary. There are Dutch Colonials and homes showing English Cottage and Spanish Revival influences. Front lawns are gracious and form a continuous green swath running the length of each block. The feeling of the entire development is one of openness, light, and air. The area is level and walking about is easy.

All five blocks front onto Hillside Avenue, where local businesses and neighborhood stores offer their goods and services. Nearby, on Francis Lewis Boulevard, about 10 blocks or half a mile away is a major shopping complex with ample parking.

The terminus of the F train is on 179th Street, about a 15-minute walk or short bus ride away. A large number of bus lines travel along Hillside Avenue, including express bus service to Manhattan and buses serving Nassau County. Travel by auto is convenient. The Clearview Expressway and the Grand Central Parkway are five minutes away and connect with a highway system that can quickly take you in any direction.

Opportunities for recreation are ample in this part of Queens. Jones Beach offers miles of superb Atlantic Ocean beaches and is only half an hour away by car. Then there is Cunningham Park, about a mile away, with 350 acres of fields, picnic areas, ballfields, and a large complex of tennis courts. About two miles away, just over the Nassau County border, is Belmont Racetrack. The racetrack is one of the finest in the country. Besides racing, the track features various musical events, as well as open-house tours of the facility during the racing season. On a different note, St. John's University, also about two miles away, offers, in addition to its regular academic programs for both day and night students, admission to student athletic events. Its basketball team, the Redmen, is highly regarded.

Real Estate

The market value of most of these nice looking homes is between $290,000 and $380,000, with a few exceptions at either end.

Transportation

HIGHWAYS: In about five minutes you can be on the Clearview Expressway heading north to the Throgs Neck Bridge, Westchester, and Connecticut, or you can be on the Grand Central Parkway heading west to Manhattan, about 30 minutes away. Almost any place in Queens can be reached in 30 minutes; LaGuardia and Kennedy airports are about 20 minutes away; Nassau County is only 10 minutes away.

SUBWAYS: The nearest subway station, the 179th Street station of the F line, requires either a short bus ride or a very long walk to get to, since it is one mile away. You can get a seat at this station, however, since the F train originates from this terminal. From 179th Street-Hillside Avenue it takes 31 minutes to Lexington Avenue-53rd Street, 36 minutes to Rockefeller Center, 37 minutes to 34th Street-Herald Square, and 44 minutes to Grand Central Station.

COMMUTER TRAINS: It is about a 10-minute walk from this area to the Long Island Rail Road Hollis Station. It takes only an additional 30 minutes to get from this station to Penn Station in Manhattan.

EXPRESS BUSES: There is a X68 express bus stop about five minutes away on Hillside Avenue and 197th Street. From there to 3rd Avenue and 51st Street or 1st Avenue and 23rd Street takes about one hour.

Shopping

Most of the local shopping is about half a mile away at, and in the vicinity of Franhil Plaza, on Hillside Avenue between 202nd and 206th Street. There are fast food, a supermarket, Chinese take-out, a bank, cleaners, and other convenience stores. There are also several stores, including pharmacies, located on Hillside Avenue between 188th and 201st streets. Additional shopping and restaurants are a few minutes away by car.

Education

ELEMENTARY SCHOOL: PS 35, grades 1-5, about 800 pupils. Located at 191-02 90th Avenue. Its reading scores place it in the top 40 percent of all public elementary schools in New York City.

INTERMEDIATE SCHOOL: IS 238, grades 6-8, is located at 88-15 182nd Street. It has about 1,600 students. Its reading scores place it in the top half of all public middle schools in New York City.

HIGH SCHOOL: The former Andrew Jackson High School building, located at 207-01 116th Avenue now houses four magnet schools, each with approximately 500 students. The schools are: Law and Government and Community Service Magnet High School; Humanities and the Arts Magnet High School; Business, Computer Applications and Entrepreneurship Magnet High School; and Mathematics, Science, Research and Technology Magnet High School. To attend, students need to apply.

Recreation

Cunningham Park, Alley Pond Park, Kissena Park, Forest Park, and Flushing Meadow Park are all five to 15 minutes away by car. For more information see PARKS in the Where To Play In Queens section.

(Also see Libraries, Private Schools, and Parochial Schools in the Appendix.)

Holliswood

(Foothill Avenue at 193rd Road to Clover Hill Drive)

A good way to experience Holliswood is to enter the community by way of Foothill Avenue. Beginning at 193rd Street, just north of Hillside Avenue, Foothill Avenue climbs a small hill, veers to the east, climbs higher, then veers to the north and continues its climb, which ends at the foot of a large glen—all the more delightful, because it is unexpected. Holliswood is like that: nestled in a glen, it has curving streets, differences in elevations, and a forest-like quality giving way to open space or possibly something else. Even the surface of Foothill Avenue is interesting. It is built of yellow brick, brick providing better traction than asphalt.

The Holliswood community immediately to the north of Foothill Avenue was built in the 1950's. What saves it from being "just another development" is the rolling topography and the heavily forested nature of the area. The result is a delightful enclave of homes set amidst different elevations and an internal, almost private, road system that discourages traffic. Like its older, luxurious counterpart, Jamaica Estates, Holliswood is built upon the highest ground in Queens, the Long Island Terminal Moraine—a gigantic hill of earth deposited by the last glacier. The moraine is part of a chain of elevated ground that includes Forest Park to the west and Prospect Park in Brooklyn.

Recreation is close by. Cunningham Park is immediately to the north of Holliswood. Its 350 acres include a tennis center, ballfields, and many open, grassy areas that are used for picnicing and sunning. At the Nassau County Line, about two miles away, is Belmont racetrack which has some of the best thoroughbred racing in the country. A mile to the west is St. John's University and its famous basketball team, the Redmen. The University has adult education and evening programs. Former New York State Governor Mario Cuomo was once on its faculty. Local shopping is found on Hillside Avenue. A mile away is the Fresh Meadows Shopping Center.

Real Estate

The few houses in the immediate area have a market value of between $300,000 and $390,000. A large house on Foothill Avenue is estimated at about $450,000.

Transportation

HIGHWAYS: In about five minutes you can be on the Clearview Expressway heading north to the Throgs Neck Bridge, Westchester, and Connecticut, or you can be on the Grand Central Parkway heading west to Manhattan, about 30 minutes away. Almost any place in Queens can be reached in 30 minutes; LaGuardia and Kennedy airports are about 20 minutes away; Nassau County is only 10 minutes away.

SUBWAYS: The nearest subway station, the 179th Street station of the F line, requires either a short bus ride or a very long walk to get to, since it is one mile away. You can get a seat at this station, however, since the F train originates from this terminal. From 179th Street-Hillside Avenue it takes 31 minutes to Lexington Avenue-53rd Street, 36 minutes to Rockefeller Center, 37 minutes to 34th Street-Herald Square, and 44 minutes to Grand Central Station.

COMMUTER TRAINS: It is about a 10-minute walk from this area to the Long Island Rail Road Hollis Station. It takes only an additional 30 minutes to get from this station to Penn Station in Manhattan.

EXPRESS BUSES: There is a X68 express bus stop about five minutes away on Hillside Avenue and 197th Street. From there, to 3rd Avenue and 51st Street or 1st Avenue and 23rd Street takes about one hour.

Shopping

Most of the local shopping is located about a half mile away at Franhill Plaza, between 202nd and 206th Street on the north side of Hillside Avenue, and at several stores located across the Plaza on the south side of the avenue. There is a large supermarket, a bank, dry cleaners, fast food, and about 20 other types of convenience stores. There are several Chinese take-out stores. There are also a few local stores on Hillside Avenue, between 188th and 201st streets. A great deal of additional shopping and restaurants are a few minutes away by car.

Education

ELEMENTARY SCHOOL: PS 35, grades 1-5, about 800 pupils. Located at 191-02 90th Avenue. Its reading scores place it in the top 40 percent of all public elementary schools in New York City.

INTERMEDIATE SCHOOL: IS 238, grades 6-8, is located at 88-15 182nd Street. It has about 1,600 students. Its reading scores place it in the top half of all public middle schools in New York City.

HIGH SCHOOL: The former Andrew Jackson High School building, located at 207-01 116th Avenue now houses four magnet schools, each with approximately 500 students. The schools are: Law and Government and Community Service Magnet High School; Humanities and the Arts Magnet High School; Business, Computer Applications and Entrepreneurship Magnet High School; and Mathematics, Science, Research and Technology Magnet High School. To attend, students need to apply.

Recreation

Alley Pond Park, Cunningham Park, Kissena Park, Forest Park, and Flushing Meadow Park are five to 15 minutes away by car. For more information see PARKS in the Where To Play In Queens section.

(Also see Libraries, Private Schools, and Parochial Schools in the Appendix.)

Jackson Heights

(37th Avenue to Northern Boulevard & 78th Street to 87th Street)

A partment house living hardly gets any better than it does in Jackson Heights. By contrast, Manhattan's Upper East Side is denser and less airy, and the Upper West Side, for all its charm, doesn't have as vibrant and eclectic a mix of people as the Heights.

The core of Jackson Heights is a 20 block area of apartment houses built in the 30 years after the Queensboro Bridge opened in 1909. To lure prospective tenants to Queens, the buildings were built to superior design standards and with added features, such as thick walls, sun parlors, dinettes, and fireplaces. Built by architects who knew what they were doing and for a clientele that craved amenities, most buildings have private courtyards, unseen from the street, that are well planted and maintained as quiet, private sitting areas. The apartment houses are architecturally distinguished—many have an English or Spanish flavor, and some blocks of houses are reminiscent of streets in London. The area has been landmarked by the city in recognition of its unique character. The four choicest blocks are 84th to 87th Streets, between 34th and 35th Avenues. There are, however, many other fine blocks among the 20 blocks comprising the landmarked area.

Shopping in Jackson Heights is a moveable feast of delights governed only by your enthusiasm and energy to explore. Thirty-seventh Avenue boasts upscale South American restaurants, bakeries, and specialty stores, as well as all the usual convenience stores. One block away is Roosevelt Avenue, which provides a melange of Central and South American, Korean, and American stores. Not far away on 74th Street is a full block of Indian stores that includes at least a half dozen restaurants and many sari shops. The shopping streets are dense with people of dozens of nationalities doing their marketing and enjoying the scores of restaurants that form a United Nations of cuisine.

For those who commute to Manhattan, the number 7 IRT train runs on elevated tracks above Roosevelt Avenue and will get you to Grand Central Station in 20 minutes.

Real Estate

According to real estate agents, prices in the notable cooperative or condominium apartment houses in the Jackson Heights Historic District fall in the following range: For a studio, $30,000 to $50,000 with a maintenance charge below $300/month; for a one-bedroom apartment, $55,000 to $90,000, with a maintenance charge from $200 to $400/month; for a two-bedroom apartment, $125,000 to $180,000, with a maintenance charge from $425 to $500/month; for a three-bedroom apartment, $185,000 to $240,000 with a maintenance charge from $450 to $800/month.

Transportation

HIGHWAYS: By using the nearby Brooklyn Queens Expressway, drivers have a choice of entering Manhattan via the Grand Central Parkway/Triborough Bridge route, or by using the Long Island Expressway/34th Street Tunnel. Either way, the trip is less than 15 minutes. LaGuardia Airport is only 10 minutes away. Thanks to a modern system of interconnected high-speed parkways and expressways, almost very point in Queens is less than a half hour away.

SUBWAYS: From the 82nd Street-Jackson Heights station of the number 7 train it is only 20 minutes to Grand Central-42nd Street, 23 minutes to 42nd Street-Times Square, 35 minutes to Brooklyn Bridge, and 35 minutes to 34th Street-Herald Square.

Shopping

This is a very large shopping area with a large number of stores, selling a wide variety of products. There are four distinct areas between 81st and 90th Streets: Roosevelt Avenue, with its large concentration of Latin American stores and restaurants; 37th Avenue, with its mixture of new Latin American enterprises and older, established, neighborhood stores; Northern Boulevard, geared to shoppers with a car, with some of the bigger video stores and supermarkets; and 82nd Street, between 37th and 40th Avenues, which is basically a street mall with more upscale shopping. A fifth area—a one-block stretch along 74th Street just north of Roosevelt Avenue—is a slice of India. There are sari shops, jewelry shops and Indian restaurants, including the Jackson Diner and the Delhi Palace. Both easily equal or surpass their Manhattan counterparts.

There are at least two dozen Latin American restaurants in the area. Colombian food predominates, but the cuisines of other Latin American countries, such as Mexico, Ecuador, and Argentina also are available. The Inti Raymi on 37th Avenue is a small Peruvian restaurant specializing in seafood. There are also Korean, Thai, and Italian restaurants, as well as several unobtrusive fast food places.

There are many bakeries, including several scrumptious Uruguayan ones that are also cafes. The area also abounds in groceries, fruit-and-vegetable stores, pharmacies, laundromats, shoe stores, supermarkets, and a vision center. All other neighborhood conveniences are available: banks, beauty parlors, candy/newspaper stores, dress shops, dry cleaners, electronics stores, florist shops, fish stores, hardware stores, health food stores, ice cream shops, nail salons, pizza parlors, and photo and pet stores.

Education

ELEMENTARY SCHOOL: PS 69, grades K-5, about 1,400 pupils. Located at 77-02 37th Avenue. Its reading scores place it in the top quarter of all public elementary schools in New York City. A new school PS 212, K-5, 34-25 82nd Street opens in fall 2000.

INTERMEDIATE SCHOOL: IS 145, J. Pulitzer Intermediate School, grades 6-8, is located at 33-34 80th Street. It has about 2,000 students, including the students in its mini-school. Its reading scores place it in the top 40 percent all public middle schools in New York City.

HIGH SCHOOL: Newtown High School is located at 48-01 90th Street. It has about 4,400 students. Over 30 percent of the students are recent immigrants, mainly Hispanic and Chinese. This is the largest percentage of immigrant students of any high

school in Queens. The school has three magnet programs that are only open to Queens residents: Major Art Program, Pre-Engineering Program, and Business Institute Program. The first two are screened programs; the school selects those students who best meet selection criteria.

Recreation

Flushing Meadow Park and Kissena Park are within 15 minutes by car. For more information see PARKS in the Where To Play In Queens section.

Thomas J. Travers Park covers two acres and is within walking distance. P.S. 148 and P.S. 149 also have playgrounds which are within walking distance.

(Also see Libraries, Private Schools, and Parochial Schools in the Appendix.)

Jamaica

(146th Street between 88th and 89th Avenues)

One hundred forty-sixth Street, between 88th and 89th Avenues, is a surprise. Situated just south of Briarwood, in the northwestern corner of Jamaica, this all but forgotten block contains a fine row of neo-Classical row houses built in 1911. The houses are sturdy and in decent condition. They have some attractive architectural features, most notably their eye-catching dormers. The row houses occupy half the block; the remainder of the block consists of detached brick homes that enrich the block and perpetuate the feeling of a bygone era.

Walking down the street, one wonders what the value of these homes would be if they were located a mile away in Richmond Hill or Kew Gardens. As they are, located in a lower middle class community, the houses offer a tremendous bargain in architectural value at pre-discovery prices. While the block appears stable and the homes maintained, it is obvious that little money has been spent to upgrade these homes to their former glory. A modest investment might yield significant changes.

Around the corner, on Sutphin Boulevard, is the Queens Court Building, a large, many columned neo-Classical structure. Hillcrest High School, a relatively modern facility built in 1971 is about half a mile away. The school offers several competitive magnet programs, one of which attracts youngsters who are interested in medical careers. The main branch of the Queens Public Library is about a mile away. This is a superb modern facility that offers almost unparalleled access to published materials. A little further afield are three colleges and a private school: York, which is part of the CUNY system and a four-year college; St. John's, a Catholic university open to all; Queens College, one of the top-rated, four-year schools in the CUNY system; and Kew-Forest, a K-12 private school. All the schools are readily accessible to mass transit. The Sutphin Avenue station of the E, F, and R trains is close by. The Lexington Avenue Station at 53rd Street in Manhattan is only 26 minutes away. The Long Island Rail Road is also close by. In 17 minutes you can be at either Flatbush Avenue in downtown Brooklyn or at Penn Station in Midtown Manhattan.

Real Estate

The market value of these stately, brick row houses which evoke an earlier era is between $180,000 and $195,000. The similarly styled, detached, single-family houses on the other side of the street are slightly more expensive.

Transportation

HIGHWAYS: The Van Wyck Expressway is only five minutes away. Using the Van Wyck, you can reach Kennedy Airport in about 10 minutes. The Van Wyck interconnects to all of the major highways in Queens. By interconnecting to the Grand Central Parkway, LaGuardia Airport is only 15 minutes away. Similar connections allow you to reach Manhattan in about 25 minutes. Almost any place in Queens can be reached in about 30 minutes, and Nassau County in only 15 minutes away.

SUBWAYS: The Sutphin Boulevard-Hillside Avenue station of the F train is one block away. From this station you can get to Grand Central Station in 36 minutes, Rockefeller Center in 40 minutes.

COMMUTER TRAINS: It is only a five-minute walk from this area to the Long Island Rail Road Jamaica Station. The Jamaica Station is the key station in the Long Island Rail Road system in Queens, because all of their train lines, with the exception of one line, stop at the Jamaica Station. There are frequent trains, many of them expresses. From Jamaica Station to Penn Station in Manhattan takes only 17 minutes. The Flatbush Avenue Station in Brooklyn is, also, only 17 minutes away.

Shopping

Most local shopping is along the three blocks on Sutphin Boulevard, between

Hillside Avenue and Jamaica Avenue with some additional shopping on Hillside Avenue and even more on Jamaica Avenue. The stores are modest and the merchandise inexpensive. There are the usual convenience stores as well as banks, several fish stores, pharmacies, liquor stores, a supermarket, and a shoe store. There are several Latin American restaurants. Additional shopping and restaurants are minutes away by car.

Education

ELEMENTARY SCHOOL: PS 82, grades 1-6, about 600 pupils. Located at 88-02 144th Street. Its reading scores place it in the top 60 percent of all public elementary schools in New York City.

JUNIOR HIGH SCHOOL: JHS 217, R.A. Van Wyck Junior High School, grades 7-8, is located at 85-05 144th Street. It has about 1,200 pupils. Its reading scores place it near the top 50 percent of all public middle schools in New York City.

HIGH SCHOOL: Hillcrest High School is located at 160-05 Highland Avenue. The school was built in 1971 and has about 3,300 students. Overall, the school is academically average. However, the overall figures hide the fact that the school offers a magnet Pre-Med and Theatre Arts Programs that attracts a core group of over 300 gifted students. In addition, a Health Careers Program attracts about 300 students.

Recreation

Forest Park and Flushing Meadow Park are both 10 minutes away by car. For more information see PARKS in the Where To Play In Queens section.

Local Park: Within a 10-minute walk is the 11.5-acre King Park on 89th Avenue.

(Also see Libraries, Private Schools, and Parochial Schools in the Appendix.)

Jamaica Estates

(Chevy Chase Street to Homelawn Street & Tudor Road to Henley Road)

Jamaica Estates is a beautiful community. Patterned after an English village, the Estates' 500 acres were laid out on gently rolling hills and heavily wooded lots. Businesses were barred and only single-family, detached houses were allowed, although, over time, some two-family homes were permitted, and apartment houses were built on the periphery of the development.

Many of the homes were built in a Tudor or colonial style, providing the eye with a harmony and symmetry not common nowadays. Many large trees, mostly oaks, were left standing, and much stone was used in the construction of the homes and in the retaining walls on the slopes. The streets are curvilinear and only a few go straight to their designated ends. The result is relatively little vehicular traffic and much peace and quiet. Most of the homes are spacious and have garages. There is ample on-street parking. Front lawns are heavily planted with rhododendrons, azaleas, and flowering trees. In spring, the Estates are ablaze with color. Since this is still a community of mostly private homes, maintenance and upkeep of the area is exceptionally high. As might be expected, the value of the homes is also high.

Transportation is good. The F train is only a few minutes walk from a large part of the Estates and is easily reached by a bus from the farthest ends of the Estates. A large number of bus lines, including buses to Nassau County, as well as a Manhattan express bus, are available on nearby Hillside Avenue. The intersection of three of the major highways in Queens—the Grand Central Parkway, the Jackie Robinson (Interboro) Parkway, and the Van Wyck Expressway—is less than five minutes away.

Cunningham Park, to the east, with its 350 acres and large tennis complex, is less than a mile away. St John's University's 105-acre campus is on the Estates' western border. Excellent public schools serve the community, while several private schools are also available, such as the United Nations International School, the Roman Catholic Mary Lewis Academy for Girls, and, less than 10 minutes away by car, the Kew-Forest School.

Real Estate

While there are some very expensive estates, the market value of most of the homes in this area ranges from just below $300,000 to about $600,000. There are nice houses with market values of about $340,000 on most of the best streets.

Transportation

HIGHWAYS: It takes only a few minutes to get onto the nearby Grand Central Parkway. Less than 30 minutes later you can be in Manhattan, or for that matter, in almost any other part of Queens. In about 15 minutes you can be at either LaGuardia Airport or Kennedy Airport. Nassau County is only 10 minutes away.

SUBWAYS: Although it takes about 15 minutes to walk to the F train station at 179th Street and Hillside Avenue, there is one big compensation: you can get a seat since the F train originates at this station. Travel times to Manhattan are: 31 minutes to Lexington Avenue-53rd Street, 36 minutes to Rockefeller Center, 37 minutes to 34th Street-Herald Square, and 44 minutes to Grand Central-42nd Street.

EXPRESS BUSES: It takes about 10 minutes to walk to the QM1 and QM1A bus stop on Union Turnpike at Utopia Parkway. Both buses are available to take you into Manhattan seven days a week. The trip to 3rd Avenue and 57th Street takes about 55 minutes.

Shopping

On Union Turnpike, between Utopia Parkway (176th Street) and 188th Street, are a wide variety of good stores and many restaurants. There is a popular diner (Fame) and restaurants featuring Italian, Japanese, Indian, Chinese, Mexican, and Israeli cuisines. Il Gibbiano was reviewed in the New York Times. Just right for casual snacks are a bagel shop/bakery, delicatessens, and pizza parlors, several of them kosher. There are also a video store, jewelry stores, dry cleaners, florists, banks, nail salons, and many beauty parlors. Also located along this commercial strip is a dance studio. Another major shopping area, the Fresh Meadows Shopping Center, is located less than a mile away.

Education

ELEMENTARY SCHOOLS: Two K-6 schools, PS 178 with about 400 pupils and PS 131 with about 800 pupils, serve this area. PS 178 is located at 189-10 Radnor Road. Its reading scores place it in the top 5 percent of all public elementary schools in New York City. PS 131 is located at 84th Avenue and 172nd Street. Its reading scores place it in the top 20 percent of all public elementary schools in New York City.

JUNIOR HIGH SCHOOL: JHS 216, G. J. Ryan Junior High School, grades 6-9, is located at 64-20 175th Street and has about 1,200 pupils. Its reading scores place it in the top 20 percent of all public middle schools in New York City.

HIGH SCHOOL: Jamaica High School is located at 167-01 Gothic Drive near the community of Jamaica Estates. Its approximately 2,500 students attend school in an architecturally imposing building built in 1927. Academically, the school's level of achievement compares favorably with the average level of achievement for all public high schools in New York City. In fact, at graduation nearly 90 percent of Jamaica students enroll in a college. The school has four magnet programs that are only open to Queens residents: Legal Studies Institute Program, Finance Institute Program, Computer Science Institute Program, and Computer in Business Program.

Recreation

Cunningham Park, Alley Pond Park, Kissena Park, Forest Park, and Flushing Meadow Park are five to 15 minutes away by car. For more information see PARKS in the Where To Play In Queens section.

(Also see Libraries, Private Schools, and Parochial Schools in the Appendix.)

Kew Gardens

(Lefferts Boulevard to Grand Central Parkway & Kew Gardens Rd. to Metropolitan Ave.)

Kew Gardens is a delightful neighborhood of Tudor- and Colonial-style homes on shady, tree-lined streets. It is nestled against the 538-acre Forest Park, yet is less than 30 minutes by train from Manhattan. Development started in 1910 when houses were marketed to Manhattanites seeking to flee the city. Kew Gardens was modeled after the fashionable London suburb of Kew Gardens, home of the London Royal Botanical Society. Like its English counterpart, the area was heavily planted with trees. Today, many of these trees are more than 75 years old and add an immeasurable degree of serenity and character to the area. The "village"—as old-timers refer to the area—has its own suburban railroad station, which also lends charm.

Kew Gardens was built at a time when labor was cheap and craftsmen were skilled, resulting in homes that are large, comfortable, and tasteful. This unique assemblage of homes offers the opportunity for gracious living within New York City. The atmosphere is friendly. Good shopping within walking distance is available on three of the four streets bounding the area (the fourth fronts Forest Park). People can easily get to know one another, especially along the Lefferts Boulevard shopping strip which contains a variety of interesting stores, as well as both family and sophisticated restaurants. The local schools are good. There is also an excellent private school nearby. Opportunities for recreation are excellent because of Forest Park which offers an 18-hole golf course, tennis courts, miles of bridle paths, two riding academies, and a restored 1895 carousel. An excellent highway network is within five minutes of the doorstep. It connects to the major roads, the two airports, and all the amenities needed for the "good life". Jones Beach and the Atlantic Ocean are just 30 minutes away by car. A five-screen art theater that shows foreign films is on Lefferts Boulevard.

The physical amenities of the area, its excellent location, and the city's low taxes make owning a home in Kew Gardens an astute investment.

Real Estate

Many of the best looking and architecturally interesting houses in the area have a market value of between $400,000 and $500,000, but there also are many other houses that are more expensive.

Transportation

HIGHWAYS: This is an ideal location from which to get to any place quickly. Only a few minutes away from this area, three major highways cross—the Grand Central Parkway, the Van Wyck Expressway, and the Jackie Robinson Parkway—allowing you to connect to other major highways. All the major entry points into Manhattan are little more than 25 minutes away. Nassau County, LaGuardia Airport, and JFK Airport are all about 15 minutes, or less, away.

SUBWAYS: Depending on exactly where one lives, it can be as much as a 15-minute walk to the Union Turnpike station located on Queens Boulevard. The station is amazingly close, however, to Manhattan. Both the E and F express trains stop at Union Turnpike. You can be at Lexington Avenue-53rd Street in 22 minutes (and with only five stops), at Rockefeller Center in 27 minutes, at Grand Central-42nd Street in 35 minutes, and Chambers Street-World Trade Center in 38 minutes. To relieve congestion on the heavily used E and F lines, a new subway connection to Manhattan is under construction and scheduled to open in the year 2002.

COMMUTER TRAINS: The Long Island Rail Road Kew Gardens station is within 10-minute walking distance of most of the homes in this area. From Kew Gardens Station to Penn Station in Manhattan takes only 17 minutes.

EXPRESS BUSES: The QM18 stops on Lefferts Boulevard and Metropolitan Avenue, Lefferts Boulevard and Austin Street, and Queens Boulevard at Hoover Street. From these stops, it takes 35 to 40 minutes to get to 3rd Avenue and 34th Street and 55 to 60 minutes to get to 3rd Avenue and 57th Street.

Shopping

The main local shopping street is Lefferts Boulevard, between Metropolitan Avenue and Austin Street. Almost as close, and still within walking distance for much of the immediate area, is Queens Boulevard, between 83rd Avenue and Union Turnpike. These two shopping streets offer a lot: bagel stores, a bakery, several banks, beauty parlors, a bicycle store, dry cleaners, a fish store, a fitness center, florists, many groceries and fruit-

and-vegetable stores, a gourmet delicatessen, laundromats, a liquor store, lots of law offices (there are courts nearby on the other side of Queens Boulevard), nail salons, pharmacies, a supermarket, video stores, and many pizza parlors. There are some good and

not overly expensive restaurants for family dining, such as Pasta Lovers and Dani's for pizza and Italian dishes. There are several other restaurants and diners serving American, Chinese, and kosher food. Additional stores and restaurants are a few minutes away by car on Queens Boulevard.

Education

ELEMENTARY SCHOOL: PS 99, grades K-6, about 1,000 pupils. Located at 82-37 Kew Gardens Road. Its reading scores place it in the top 15 percent of all public elementary schools in New York City.

JUNIOR HIGH SCHOOL: JHS 190, Russell Sage Junior High School, grades 7-9, is located at 68-17 Austin Street. It has about 1,400 students. Its reading scores place it near the top 15 percent of all public middle schools in New York City.

HIGH SCHOOL: Hillcrest High School is located at 160-05 Highland Avenue. The school was built in 1971 and has about 3,300 students. Overall, the school is academically average in comparison to other high schools in the New York City school system. However, the overall figures hide the fact that the school offers a magnet Pre-Med Program that attracts a core group of over 200 academically gifted students. This program (and the school's Theatre Arts Program, which has over 100 students) is a screened program; the school selects those students who best meet selection criteria. In addition there is a Health Careers Program that attracts about 300 students.

Recreation

Forest Park: You can walk to the park in 10 minutes; other parts can be reached by car in five minutes; Flushing Meadow Park is not far, less than 10 minutes away by car. For more information on these parks see PARKS in the Where To Play In Queens section.

(Also see Libraries, Private Schools, and Parochial Schools in the Appendix.)

Kew Gardens–Park Lane South

(Curzon, Grosvenor, and Mayfair Roads between Park Lane South and 116th St)

Three small blocks of charming homes open onto Park Lane South and the 538-acre expanse called Forest Park across the street. All three—Grosvenor Road, Mayfair Road, and Curzon Road—are well located to take advantage of Forest Park's amenities. They are close to public schools as well as to good private schools, such as the Kew-Forest School. Good shopping and dining are nearby, too, and an extensive highway network, only minutes away, quickly and easily connects the private world of Park Lane South to Long Island, Manhattan, Westchester, and Brooklyn.

These three streets are special for several reasons. Their size is small, with maybe a dozen homes on each street. Each block is private, due to an uphill grade towards Park Lane South and the lack of through traffic. And finally, there is an enormous and usable park only a few hundred feet from every home.

Residents of these blocks can easily walk to either Metropolitan Avenue for a wide range of shopping and some casual neighborhood restaurants, or a bit further to Lefferts Boulevard. Lefferts Boulevard takes on a village-like atmosphere as it winds through Kew Gardens. Many of the buildings are Tudor style. There is even a quaint railroad station where you can get the Long Island Railroad which whisks you to Manhattan in 17 minutes. There are a number of small ethnic restaurants, a bicycle store, a five-screen movie theater, and several temples situated on, or immediately off, Lefferts Boulevard.

Forest Park contains a host of amenities that are difficult to find, especially in such variety, elsewhere in New York City: There is horseback riding available at two stables on the north side of the park; there are trails, and roadways which are used exclusively by bicyclists on the weekends; there are tennis courts, baseball fields, softball fields, and playgrounds; there is an 18-hole golf course; and lastly, there are a wonderful old carousel and a band shell which has free outdoor concerts in the summer.

Real Estate

The market value of houses in this small area vary considerably, depending on whether the home is a mini-mansion or simply a pleasant Tudor-style house. In general, market values range between $450,000 and $800,000, with homes at the lower end of the scale being more prevalent.

Transportation

HIGHWAYS: This is an ideal location from which to get to any place quickly. Only a few minutes away from this area, three major highways cross—the Grand Central Parkway, the Van Wyck Expressway, and the Jackie Robinson Parkway—allowing you to connect to other major highways, All the major entry points into Manhattan are little more than 25 minutes away. Nassau County, LaGuardia Airport, and JFK Airport are all about 15 minutes, or less, away.

SUBWAYS: Depending on exactly where one lives, it can be as much as a 15-minute walk to the Union Turnpike station located on Queens Boulevard. The station is amazingly close, however, to Manhattan. Both the E and F express trains stop at Union Turnpike. You can be at Lexington Avenue-53rd Street in 22 minutes (and with only five stops), at Rockefeller Center in 27 minutes, at Grand Central-42nd Street in 35 minutes, and Chambers Street-World Trade Center in 38 minutes. To relieve congestion on the heavily used E and F lines, a new subway connection to Manhattan is under construction and scheduled to open in the year 2002.

COMMUTER TRAINS: The Long Island Rail Road Kew Gardens station is within 10 minutes walking distance of most of the homes in this area. From Kew Gardens Station to Penn Station in Manhattan takes only 17 minutes.

EXPRESS BUSES: The QM18 stops on Lefferts Boulevard and Metropolitan Avenue, Lefferts Boulevard and Austin Street, and Queens Boulevard at Hoover Street. From these stops, it takes 35 to 40 minutes to get to 3rd Avenue and 34th Street and 55 to 60 minutes to get to 3rd Avenue and 57th Street.

Shopping

The nearest shopping street is Metropolitan Avenue between Park Lane South and Lefferts Boulevard. All the everyday necessities can be found here: a supermarket, banks, groceries, laundromats, beauty parlors, dry cleaners, liquor stores, pharmacies, pizza parlors, Chinese take-outs, and video stores. There is also a steak house/bar, an Italian restaurant (Spolinis), and an old fashioned ice cream store (Metro Soda Fountain). A lot of additional shopping is literally less than two minutes away by car.

Education

ELEMENTARY SCHOOL: PS 90, grades K-6, about 1,200 pupils. Located at 86-50 109th Street. Its reading scores place it in the top 60 percent of all public elementary schools in New York City.

JUNIOR HIGH SCHOOL: Junior High School 226, grades 7-8, is located at 121-10 Rockaway Boulevard. It has about 1,900 students. Its reading scores place it in the top 50 percent of all public middle schools in New York City.

HIGH SCHOOL: Richmond Hill High School is located at 89-30 114th Street. It has about 3,200 students. Nearly one-fourth of the students are recent immigrants; Spanish and Russian are the two largest language groups of students with limited English proficiency. Approximately 20 percent of students take and pass advanced placement (college credit) courses, a percentage much higher than the average high school. The school has a Business Institute magnet program that is only open to Queens residents.

Recreation

Forest Park is nearby; parts of it can be walked to, the rest is about a five-minute drive away. Flushing Meadow Park is within a 10-minute drive. For more information about these parks see PARKS in the Where To Play In Queens section.

(Also see Libraries, Private Schools, and Parochial Schools in the Appendix.)

Laurelton

(228th Street from Mentone Street to 135th Avenue)

Why live on Long Island and pay real estate taxes that are often two to three times higher than New York City when you could live in Queens and have all the advantages of Long Island? On 228th Street in Laurelton, between Mentone and 135th Avenues, are several pleasant suburban blocks with more pluses than most. These include: a strong civic association; a center mall cared for by the community; a mix of housing types; a suburban railway station within walking distance; an 89-acre park, with a pond, trees, and grass within a half mile; and immediate access to the Southern State Parkway, Cross Island Parkway, and the Sunrise Highway. The area is also close to superbly maintained Atlantic Ocean beaches including Jones Beach, less than 30 minutes away by car; Belmont Racetrack, about 10 minutes away by car; and just a few minutes by car to the famous Green Acres Shopping Center. If you choose to go into Manhattan the LIRR gets you to Penn Station in 25 minutes.

The Laurelton community is part of a large area of private homes that takes its character from the Long Island communities immediately to its east. Valley Stream, Long Island, is literally next door. To the southeast are Rosedale, Queens, and Woodmere, one of the so called Five Towns of Long Island. And nothing could be more Long Island than the Green Acres Shopping Center, with its scores of stores and acres of parking.

If the suburban life is for you, the area's relatively low home prices and taxes provide an attractive alternative to Long Island. In Laurelton, any disadvantages of being part of New York City are far outweighed by the advantages.

Real Estate

The market value of the houses on 228th Street which comprise this area range from $140,000 for an attractive brick row house to between $210,000 and $280,000 for a detached, single-family home.

Transportation

HIGHWAYS: Although located in the extreme southeastern part of Queens, almost on the Nassau County border, this area is but five minutes from two modern highways: the Cross Island Parkway and the Southern State/Belt Parkway. Thus, not only is Nassau

County five minutes away and Kennedy Airport 10 minutes away, but anyplace in Queens can be reached in about 30 minutes. Manhattan is, also, about 30 minutes distant.

SUBWAYS: There are no subways nearby. To get to the closest subway station, Jamaica Center, the terminus of the E, J, and Z lines, requires walking a moderate distance to a bus stop on either Merrick Boulevard or North Conduit Avenue, and an approximately 20-minute bus ride to Jamaica Center. From Jamaica Center to Lexington Avenue-53rd Street takes 28 minutes, to Penn Station-34th Street takes 35 minutes, to the World Trade Center takes 44 minutes, and it takes 46 minutes to get to Broadway-Nassau-Fulton Streets in Lower Manhattan.

COMMUTER TRAINS: From the nearby Laurelton Station on the LIRR Far Rockaway line to Penn Station in Manhattan is a trip of 31 minutes. To get to the Flatbush Avenue Station in Brooklyn takes even less time, only 25 minutes.

EXPRESS BUSES: The X63 express bus stops on Merrick Boulevard, about a 10- to 15-minute walk away. The bus will take you to 1st Avenue and 23rd Street in Manhattan in about 60 minutes.

Shopping

The closest shopping street serving this area is Merrick Boulevard. Most stores are located between Springfield Boulevard and 236th Street. While there are not any fancy restaurants, there are plenty of local retail stores. These include three supermarkets, several bakeries, some laundromats, and beauty parlors, a bank, a liquor store, a nail salon, groceries, a pharmacy, a florist, and a dry cleaners. There are some West Indian stores, including a bakery, and Chinese take-outs. Green Acres Shopping Center, one of the largest shopping centers on Long Island, is only five minutes away by car.

Education

ELEMENTARY SCHOOL: PS 156, grades K-6, about 900 pupils. Located at 229-02 137th Avenue. Its reading score places it in the top 40 percent of all public elementary schools in New York City.

INTERMEDIATE SCHOOL: IS 231, Tri Community Intermediate School, grades 7-8, is located at 145-00 Springfield Boulevard. It has about 1,600 students. Its reading scores place it near the top 50 percent of all public middle schools in New York City.

HIGH SCHOOL: Springfield Gardens High School is located at 143-10 Springfield Boulevard. It has 2,000 students. The school needs to be improved academically, a lower than average percent of its students plan to go on to a four-year college. The school's emphasis, however, is vocational/technical training combined with a strong academic foundation. The school has four magnet programs only open to Queens residents: Veterinary Science Program, Business Technology Institute, Food Service Institute, and Law Institute.

Recreation

Alley Pond Park and Cunningham Park are 15 minutes away by car. For more information on these parks see PARKS in the Where To Play In Queens section.

Local Parks: Brookville Park, covering 89 acres, and Springfield Park, covering 23 acres, are located on Brookville and Springfield Boulevards, respectively. Each is only five minutes away by car. They are both pretty parks, built along stream valleys, and each has tennis courts, play facilities, and a pond.

(Also see Libraries, Private Schools, and Parochial Schools in the Appendix.)

Long Island City

(45th Avenue between 21st and 23rd Streets)

Imagine a block of brownstones from one of the better brownstone neighborhoods of Manhattan or Brooklyn lifted up and transported intact to Queens within sight of the East River and the Manhattan skyline. Such a block actually exists, and it is the only one like it in Queens. This block is Forty-Fifth Avenue between 21st and 23rd Streets. On it are examples of the city's best preserved Italianate row houses, as well as homes of French Empire, neo-Grecian, and Queen Anne styles.

Everywhere you look, the eye is treated to a display of post Civil War craftsmanship, from carved stone and wrought iron details to staircases constructed in a grand manner, rising opulently from the street to the second floor doorway entrances. Light fixtures of turn-of-the-century vintage are affixed to many buildings. The whole block has a sense of unity and character.

Adding to the charm of the block is the fact that in the immediate vicinity are several interesting buildings including: P.S. 1, a former public school built in 1892 in Romanesque Revival style and turned into an art museum/artist's studio space; the bold green glass, ultra modern hi-rise tower of the CitiBank office building; the architecturally distinguished Queens County Courthouse; Silvercup Studios, a former bakery converted into a major film and television production facility; and a surrounding neighborhood of mostly low-rise, human-scale buildings where light, air, and openness are abundant. A two-and-a-half acre playground is located on 21st Avenue, at the foot of the block.

If you use the subway, you have a choice of four lines within a 5-minute walk of this unique block. One of them will get you into Manhattan in 3 minutes!

Real Estate

Based on recent sales, the market value of these handsome, one-and-two family, 1870's brownstones is between $320,000 and $400,000. This block is part of the Hunters Point Historic District.

Transportation

HIGHWAYS: Manhattan is an unbelievable five minutes away via the 59th Street/Queensboro Bridge. And it costs nothing to use. Or take the Queens Midtown Tunnel and enter Manhattan at 36th Street in less than 10 minutes, although there is a tunnel fee. The Long Island Expressway is nearby and actually is an express highway at this point as it heads eastward. Interconnections with other highways allow you to get to almost any part of Queens in a half hour. And LaGuardia Airport is only 15 minutes away.

SUBWAYS: Both the E and F trains and the number 7 train are nearby. By using the 23rd Street-Ely Avenue-Court Square station, or the 45th Road-Court House Square station, you can reach almost any important Manhattan destination in a few minutes. For example, Lexington Avenue-53rd Street is three minutes away, Grand Central Station is six minutes away, 47-50th Street-Rockefeller Center is seven minutes away, and 42nd Street-Times Square is 10 minutes away. It doesn't get much better than this.

Shopping

There is convenience shopping in the immediate vicinity, as well as a supermarket, several groceries, a fruit-and-vegetable store, a dry cleaner, a deli/grocery, a florist, a meat market, and a bank. There are a few local restaurants and a Chinese take-out. The Court Square Diner has superior diner food and the most delicious custard flan this side of Spain. It's made fresh several times a week and is best eaten out of the custard dish. A much greater array of stores is available in Sunnyside, about five minutes away by car, or in Astoria, less than 10 minutes by car.

Education

ELEMENTARY SCHOOL: PS 76, grades pre-K-5, about 800 pupils. Located at 36-36 10th Street. Its reading scores place it near the top 50 percent of all elementary schools in New York City.

JUNIOR HIGH SCHOOL: JHS 204, O. W. Holmes Junior High School, grades 6-8, is located at 36-41 28th Street. It has about 1,200 students. Its reading scores place it near the top 40 percent of all public middle schools in New York City.

HIGH SCHOOL: Long Island City High School is located at 14-30 Broadway; this newly built school opened in 1995 and has about 3,300 pupils. The school uses the latest and most advanced technology (computers, internet, CD-Rom, etc.) as a foundation for learning. The school has an athletic field and a swimming pool. Long Island City High School has two magnet programs that are only open to Queens residents: Technology and the Arts Program and Culinary Institute Program. These are screened programs; the school selects those students who best meet selection criteria.

Recreation

Queensbridge Park: This 20-acre park, just north of the Queensboro Bridge, faces the East River and Roosevelt Island. It is a 15-minute walk away.

John F. Murray Playground covers two acres and is less than a 5-minute walk away.

Forest Park. This 538-acre gem is about 15 minutes away by car. For more information about this park see PARKS in the Where To Play In Queens section.

(Also see Libraries, Private Schools, and Parochial Schools in the Appendix.)

Malba

(10th Avenue to Powells Cove & 138th Street to Parsons Boulevard)

Luxury looms large in this 10 block pocket of affluence at the northernmost tip of Queens. This triangular shape area, bounded by the well hidden approaches to the Whitestone Bridge on the east, by 12th Avenue on the south, and by Long Island Sound on the west, offers some of the most conspicuously luxurious homes in the city. Set in a safe cul-de-sac, seemingly untroubled by the tensions that interlace living in the city, these immaculate looking homes face onto wide streets that are curvilinear to discourage traffic that doesn't belong.

Many homes have views of the blue or grey waters of Long Island Sound (the color depends on the sun and sky) as well as a dramatic view of the Whitestone Bridge. At the north tip of Malba, sitting on the edge of the Sound, is 16-acre Francis Lewis Park. It features a grassy strand perfect for picnicing and relaxation, with beautiful views of this graceful bridge.

A car is a necessity in Malba, because there is no subway and only one bus line which runs along 14th Avenue. There are no local shopping streets or convenience stores either within easy walking distance. Fortunately, a large shopping center is only a mile away in Whitestone, and downtown Flushing, which is one of New York City's largest shopping districts outside of Manhattan, is less than 10 minutes away. Downtown Flushing is also the home of dozens of varied and highly rated Asian restaurants. As such, it has become a culinary rival to Manhattan's better known Chinatown.

In addition, access to all major roads of the Queens' expressway and parkway system is literally at Malba's doorstep, allowing quick and easy trips to the rest of the borough, Manhattan, and Long Island.

Real Estate

Based on the most recent information, the market value of houses in the most desirable part of this community of beautiful homes—on and along Malba Drive—range from $750,000 to well over $2 million. Less luxurious and less expensive homes can be found nearby, on Parsons Boulevard, beginning around $400,000.

Transportation

HIGHWAYS: Malba sits astride the Whitestone Bridge and Whitestone Expressway, so it's possible to be in Manhattan, via the Triborough Bridge, in about 20 minutes, or across the Whitestone Bridge and into Connecticut in about the same amount of time. Almost anyplace in Queens is 30 minutes or less away; LaGuardia Airport is only 15 minutes away; Nassau County is little more than 10 minutes distant.

SUBWAYS: There are no nearby subways. The closest subway station is the 7 line station at Main Street in Flushing, which requires a long walk to a bus stop and an approximately 20-minute ride, exclusive of waiting time. From the Main Street Station to Grand Central Station is a 26-minute subway ride.

EXPRESS BUSES: Depending on exactly where in Malba you live, it may take 15 minutes to walk to the QM2 bus stop at 14th Avenue and the Whitestone Expressway. From there, however, to 3rd Avenue and 57th Street in Manhattan takes approximately 40 minutes if there are no undue delays.

Shopping

There is no shopping within walking distance. There are, however, two shopping areas within five minutes. The larger of the two is the Whitestone Shopping district, consisting of over 60 stores between 12th and 14th Avenues on 150th Street. The second, newer, shopping area, at 20th Avenue and 132nd Street, has a large supermarket and bakery, national chain stores, and plenty of parking.

Education

ELEMENTARY SCHOOL: PS 79, grades K-6, about 1,000 pupils. Located at 15-28 149th Street. Its reading scores place it in the top 10 percent of all public elementary schools in New York City.

JUNIOR HIGH SCHOOL: JHS 194, W. H. Carr Junior High School, grades 7-9, is located at 154-60 17th Avenue. It has about 900 students. Its reading scores place it in the top 15 percent of all public middle schools in New York City.

HIGH SCHOOL: Flushing High School is located at 35-01 Union Street. It has about 2,200 pupils, a smaller student body than most New York City High Schools. A third of the students have limited proficiency in English and a quarter of the students are recent immigrants, with Hispanics and Koreans the two largest groups. The school has the Thurgood Marshall Law Academy magnet program that is only open to Queens residents. This program is selective; about 25 percent of the students that applied were accepted.

Recreation

Flushing Meadow Park, Alley Pond Park, Cunningham Park, and Kissena Park are all about 15 minutes away by car. Francis Lewis Park is within walking distance. For more information about these parks see PARKS in the Where To Play In Queens section.

(Also see Libraries, Private Schools, and Parochial Schools in the Appendix.)

PRIVATE
PROPERTY
NO
TRESPASSING

84-10-20 101 ST

Park Lane South Condominiums

Richmond Hill–Condo

(84-10 & 84-20 101st Street corner of Park Lane South)

In the last quarter of the 19th Century a number of factories, of the type that abound in New England, were built in Queens. A hundred years later almost all traces of these buildings have disappeared. But in Richmond Hill, one extremely good example of the type survived long enough to become part of the residential condominium boom of the 1980's. This former briarwood pipe factory has been converted into a handsome, four-story brick structure of 87 apartments, boasting thick walls and high ceilings. Parking is available and plentiful on the site's central mall.

The building is situated at 84-10 101st Street, across the street from the 538-acre Forest Park. The park is wooded and sits on one of the highest points in the borough, atop the terminal moraine deposited here 10,000 years ago by a glacier. The park has an 18-hole golf course, tennis courts, bicycle paths, a carousel, sport fields, bridle paths for horseback riding, and playgrounds. A playground is one block away.

Immediately to the east of the condominium, especially along 86th Avenue between 104th and 116th Streets, are many architecturally interesting residences dating from the turn of the century. At, or near, 117th Street, in the vicinity of Hillside Avenue and about a 15-minute walk from 101st Street, are a 1905 Carnegie library, the Landmark Tavern Building, and Frank Jahn's 1890 ice cream parlor.

While adequate convenience shopping is nearby, a car easily brings more varied shopping opportunities and all of the other attractions of neighboring Kew Gardens, Forest Hills, and Woodhaven within five minutes of the condominium's doorstep. Train service to Manhattan is a short walk away. The ride on the J/Z line elevated subway to Chambers Street in Lower Manhattan takes 36 minutes. The ride to Rockefeller Center takes 50 minutes.

Real Estate

The prices of units in this building, after falling considerably during the slump of the late 1980's, have now increased substantially. Currently, a one-bedroom apartment costs between $90,000 and $125,000, with a $180/month maintenance charge, while a two-bedroom apartment costs between $120,000 and $175,000, with a maintenance charge of $220/month. There are a small number of three-bedroom apartments for about $185,000, with maintenance of $250/month. However, prices are changing rapidly.

Transportation

HIGHWAYS: Woodhaven Boulevard, a nearby, major Queens thoroughfare, provides access within 10 minutes to the Long Island Expressway and the Jackie Robinson Parkway to the north and the Belt Parkway to the south. Manhattan is less than a half-hour away. Nassau County is less than 25 minutes away, and JFK Airport and LaGuardia Airport are each about 15 minutes away.

SUBWAYS: The 104-102 Street J train station is within easy walking distance. From this station it is only 36 minutes to Brooklyn Bridge-Chambers Street, 39 minutes to Broad Street, 42 minutes to Lexington Avenue-53rd Street, and 50 minutes to Rockefeller Center.

EXPRESS BUSES: While there are no express buses immediately nearby, if you are willing to walk 10 to 15 minutes, you can reach the QM18 on Lefferts Boulevard and Jamaica Avenue, or the QM15, QM16, QM17, and QM23 on Woodhaven Boulevard at either Jamaica Avenue or at Forest Park Drive. While it takes about an hour on any of these buses to get to 3rd Avenue and 57th Street, the QM23 will take you to Penn Station in about 40 minutes, barring traffic delays.

Shopping

The local shopping street is Jamaica Avenue, between 99th Street and 93rd Street (Woodhaven Boulevard). A bank, a bakery, a delicatessen, a dry cleaners, several groceries, a hardware store, several laundromats, a liquor store, a meat market, a nail salon, a tiny Thai and small Peruvian restaurant, a pizza parlor, a shoe repair store, a video store, a supermarket, and assorted other stores take care of most everyday needs. Approximately a mile away at Woodhaven Boulevard and Atlantic Avenue is a large shopping center that provides additional stores and variety.

Education

ELEMENTARY SCHOOL: PS 66, grades K-6, about 400 pupils. Located at 85-11 102nd Street. Its reading scores place it in the top 30 percent of all public elementary schools in New York City.

JUNIOR HIGH SCHOOL: Junior High School 210, E. Blackwell Junior High School, grades 7-8, is located at 93-11 101st Street. It has about 2,100 pupils. Its reading scores place it near the top 40 percent of all middle schools in New York City.

HIGH SCHOOL: Richmond Hill High School is located at 89-30 114th Street. It has about 3,200 students. Nearly one-fourth of the students are recent immigrants; Spanish and Russian are the two largest language groups of students with limited English proficiency. Approximately 20 percent of students take and pass advanced placement (college credit) courses, a percentage much higher than the average for all high schools in New York City. The School has a Business Institute magnet program that is only open to Queens residents.

Recreation

Forest Park: This 538-acre gem is across the street. Flushing Meadow Park is 15 minutes away by car. For more information see PARKS in the Where To Play In Queens section.

(Also see Libraries, Private Schools, and Parochial Schools in the Appendix.)

Richmond Hill North

(Park Lane South to Jamaica Avenue & 105th Street to 112th Street)

Richmond Hill, especially the northern part between South Park Lane, Jamaica Avenue, 104th, and 114th Streets, is a residential area of Victorian and Queen Anne style houses that has managed to escape the developer's wrecking ball and still maintains its charm due to good planning, good architecture, and a strong neighborhood association. Patterned after the London suburb of the same name, the American Richmond Hill was created as a garden suburb offering easy access to Manhattan.

The area's northern boundry is literally a forest, with hills and glens dating back to the last ice age. Today, these woods are known as Forest Park and their 538 acres contain not only trees and hiking trails, but an 18-hole golf course, tennis courts, ballfields, bridal paths used by two nearby riding academies, a carousel, and an outdoor bandshell that features live performances in the summer. The sense of trees and woods pervades Richmond Hill, too, with leafy canopies forming cool tunnels of green to shade the streets from the summer sun.

Turn of the century architecture predominates. Homes have either porches or columned facades, as well as details such as stained glass windows, ornamental gingerbread trim, balconies, odd turrets, dormers, and gambrel roofs. This visual feast reflects a time when rich German merchants first settled in Richmond Hill in the 1880's. Traces of this other time can still be found in the area, including the former Triangle Hofbrau on Myrtle Avenue and 117th Street, which dates from 1864 and Frank Jahn's 1890's ice cream parlor. Other notable buildings include a mint-condition Carnegie Library, built in 1904, and the Landmark Tavern Building, built around 1900.

In 1972 The Richmond Hill Block Association was organized to fight the attempts of some real estate brokers to blockbust the neighborhood. The Association succeeded, and today it's a force guarding real estate values and providing cooperative endeavors that range from fix-up workshops to block parties.

For those who must get into Manhattan, Wall Street is 41 minutes away by elevated subway. A 10-minute bus ride to the Long Island Rail Road's Kew Gardens Station gets you to Penn Station in an additional 17 minutes.

Real Estate

The market value of these large old houses with their imposing presence, many bedrooms, large oak-lined interiors, and two-car garages varies by block; however, prices generally range from $260,000 to $320,000. Where previous owners have done some renovation, or if there are special amenities, prices start at $350,000.

Transportation

HIGHWAYS: Woodhaven Boulevard, a nearby, major, Queens thoroughfare, provides access within 10 minutes to the Long Island Expressway and the Jackie Robinson Parkway to the north and the Belt Prkway to the south. Manhattan is less than a half-hour away. Nassau County is less than 25 minutes away and JFK Airport and LaGuardia Airport are each about 15 minutes away.

SUBWAYS: The 104-102 Street J train station is within easy walking distance. From this station it is only 36 minutes to Brooklyn Bridge-Chambers Street, 39 minutes to Broad Street, 42 minutes to Lexington Avenue-53rd Street, and 50 minutes to Rockefeller Center.

EXPRESS BUSES: While there are no express buses immediately nearby, if you are willing to walk 10 to 15 minutes, you can reach the QM18 on Lefferts Boulevard and Jamaica Avenue, or the QM15, QM16, QM17, and QM23 on Woodhaven Boulevard at either Jamaica Avenue or at Forest Park Drive. While it takes about an hour on any of these buses to get to 3rd Avenue and 57th Street, the QM23 will take you to Penn Station in about 40 minutes, barring traffic delays.

Shopping

The local shopping street is Jamaica Avenue, between 99th Street and 93rd Street (Woodhaven Boulevard). A bank, a bakery, a delicatessen, a dry cleaners, several groceries, a hardware store, several laundromats, a liquor store, a meat market, a nail salon, a tiny Thai and small Peruvian restaurant, a pizza parlor, a shoe repair store, a video store, a supermarket, and assorted other stores take care of most everyday needs. Approximately a mile away at Woodhaven Boulevard and Atlantic Avenue is a large shopping center that provides additional stores and variety.

Education

ELEMENTARY SCHOOL: Two K-6 schools, PS 66, grades K-6, about 400 pupils, and PS 90 with about 1,200 pupils, serve this area. PS 66 is located at 85-11 102nd Street. Its reading scores place it in the top 30 percent of all public elementary schools in New York City. PS 90 is located at 86-50 109th Street. Its reading scores place it in the top 60 percent of all public elementary schools in New York City.

JUNIOR HIGH: Two junior high schools, grades 7-8, serve this area. Junior High School 210, E. Blackwell Junior High School, grades 7-8, is located at 93-11 101st Street. It has about 2,100 pupils. Junior High School 226 is located at 121-10 Rockaway Boulevard. It has 1,900 students. Reading scores at both schools place them near the top 40 to 50 percent of all public middle schools in New York City.

HIGH SCHOOL: Richmond Hill High School is located at 89-30 114th Street. It has about 3,200 students. Nearly one-fourth of the students are recent immigrants; Spanish and Russian are the largest language groups of students with limited English proficiency. Approximately 20 percent of students take and pass advanced placement courses, a percentage much higher than the average for all high schools in New York City. The School has a Business Institute magnet program that is only open to Queens residents.

Recreation

Forest Park is a short walk away. Flushing Meadow Park is 15 minutes away by car. For more information see PARKS in the Where To Play In Queens section.

(Also see Libraries, Private Schools, and Parochial Schools in the Appendix,)

Ridgewood–Sixty-Ninth Avenue

(69th Avenue between Fresh Pond Road and 60th Street)

On 69th Avenue, between 60th Street and Fresh Pond Road, are two distinct blocks with a lot of character. One block is a sea of porches and narrow columns and the other of brownstone stoops and three-story "brickstone" houses. On parts of these streets trees form a leafy canopy, perfect for summertime porch and stoop sitting. The two blocks have a high degree of architectural cohesion and a distinct feeling of place and of a time which dates back to the beginning of the 20th Century. But this isn't at all surprising, considering that these blocks are located in Ridgewood, which has the largest concentration of districts in the United States on the National Register of Historic Places.

Ridgewood has a German heritage, which is apparent in the thousands of solidly constructed, three-story, yellow brick row houses that line its streets, as well as in the butcher shops, restaurants, and chocolate and candy stores that are scattered throughout the neighborhood, especially on Myrtle Avenue.

Myrtle Avenue is a major shopping street with over 300 community businesses. The street was revitalized in the early 1980's with federal grants, city money, and funds from local businessmen. Trees were planted, new sidewalks built, streets repaved, and street furniture added. The street offers a wide variety of shopping and is a commercial anchor for the community. Additional shopping and restaurants are found literally around the corner on Fresh Pond Road. And if that weren't enough, about a mile away is Metro Mall with its more than two dozen stores.

While the unity of buildings and the feeling of neighborhood is readily apparent to even the short-term visitor, the City is not far away. Manhattan's Fulton Street is a 28-minute train ride away, and Grand Central Station is a 35-minute trip. For either destination take the M train, and you'll always get a seat to the City.

Real Estate

Based on recent sales, the market value of the two-story, two-family brick houses with porches ranges from $200,000 to $235,000; the cost of the two-story, three-family brick houses with brownstone stoops ranges from $240,000 to $270,000.

Transportation

HIGHWAYS: In less than 15 minutes you can be on either the Long Island Expressway or the Brooklyn-Queens Expressway, and in less than 10 additional minutes, either in Midtown Manhattan or Lower Manhattan. The Jackie Robinson Parkway is even closer, less than 10 minutes away. It will take you into Brooklyn, or via the Grand Central Parkway, out to Eastern Queens, as well as to Nassau and Suffolk counties via the Northern State Parkway.

SUBWAYS: From the Fresh Pond station of the M train to Brooklyn Bridge-Chambers Street takes 28 minutes, to Broadway-Nassau-Fulton takes 30 minutes, to Grand Central-42nd Street takes 38 minutes, and to Rockefeller Center takes 51 minutes.

EXPRESS BUSES: The QM24 and the QM24W buses stop at Fresh Pond Road and Catalpa Avenue, very close to this area. The QM24W will take you to the Wall Street area in about 45 minutes, barring any traffic delays. The QM24 will take you to 34th Street and 3rd Avenue in 40 minutes and to 59th Street and 3rd Avenue in 55 minutes.

Shopping

There are two shopping streets: Myrtle Avenue and Fresh Pond Road. They both have scores of convenience stores for everyday necessities, as well as specialty stores such as a home made chocolate shop. There are pharmacies, bagel shops, pizza parlors, and Chinese take-outs, as well as German and Italian restaurants. Many banks and a super-market serve the area. Metro Mall is three minutes away by car. It has about two dozen stores.

Education

ELEMENTARY SCHOOL: PS 88, grades K-5, about 1,700 pupils. Located at 60-85 Catalpa Avenue. Its reading scores place it in the top 60 percent of all public elementary schools in New York City.

INTERMEDIATE SCHOOL: IS 93, Ridgewood Intermediate School, grades 6-8, is located at 66-56 Forest Avenue. It has about 1,600 students. Its reading scores place it in the top 40 percent of all public middle schools in New York City.

HIGH SCHOOL: Franklin K. Lane High School is located at 999 Jamaica Avenue. It has about 3,100 students. Student achievement test scores are below the average. The school has three magnet programs: Law, Pre-Engineering, and Optometry.

Recreation

Forest Park and Flushing Meadow Park are, respectively, five to 15 minutes away by car. For more information see PARKS in the Where To Play In Queens section.

Joseph Mafera Park, 5.4 acres, is less than a 10-minute walk away on 68th Place.

(Also see Libraries, Private Schools, and Parochial Schools in the Appendix.)

Ridgewood–Stockholm Street

(Stockholm Street between Onderdonk and Woodward Avenues)

Charm lives on a yellow brick street. At one end of this street is the enveloping presence of a 165-foot high, twin-towered neo-Renaissance Roman Catholic church. At the other end is the low stone wall of the small, historic Linden Hill cemetery (no longer in active use). The street, itself, is lined on either side by columned houses. Nearly every house on the block has a porch. All of this creates a unity that is seldom found on blocks in New York City.

So distinct is the street that the thought enters the mind that the residents must know one another; that they must throw block party after block party, so drawn together are they by the brick of the street.

The houses are two story and have rounded bay windows and interesting iron stoop railings that, along with the seemingly endless rows of columns, give the block its harmonious feeling.

While the immediate area contains its share of nondescript houses, there is also a large concentration of yellow brick, two- and three-story row houses and tenements that were included in the National Register of Historic Places in 1983. In fact, this area of Queens known as Ridgewood has one of the largest concentrations of historic places in the United States.

Adequate parking exists on the block, which is a good thing since local convenience stores, while handy, are insufficient for the full range of needs. Fortunately, a giant shopping complex called Metro Mall is little more than five minutes away by car, as is the large, busy, and varied Myrtle Avenue shopping district.

The L train is a few blocks away, and it is only a 17-minute ride to Union Square in Manhattan. Within a five-minute walk of Stockholm Street is a five-acre park with a playground and green, open space. Onderdonck House, a restored early 18th Century Dutch Colonial farmhouse, is 10 minutes away.

Real Estate

Based on recent sales, the market value of a house in this row of harmonious white-columned, two-family homes is between $200,000 and $230,000.

Transportation

HIGHWAYS: It may take about 10 minutes of traveling on local streets to get onto the Long Island Expressway or the Brooklyn-Queens Expressway, but once you are on these roads you can reach Lower Manhattan via the Williamsburg Bridge in another five minutes or, in a few more minutes, you can be at 36th Street via the Midtown Tunnel. Almost anyplace in Queens in about 30 minutes away by car.

SUBWAYS: While it may take 10 or 15 minutes to walk to the closest subway station, it takes only 17 minutes to travel from the DeKalb Avenue station of the L line to 14th Street-Union Square in Manhattan. The slightly more distant Seneca Avenue station of the M line is especially good for Lower Manhattan travelers. Brooklyn Bridge-Chambers Street is 25 minutes away and the Broadway-Nassau-Fulton Street station is 27 minutes away. Other important destinations, such as Grand Central-42nd Street and Lexington Avenue-59th Street are both 35 minutes away.

Shopping

The immediate neighborhood provides basic conveniences: grocery stores and a small supermarket. Less than five minutes away by car is Myrtle Avenue with its many shops and Metro Mall with two dozen stores selling everything from toys to fast food.

Education

ELEMENTARY SCHOOL: PS 81, grades K-5, about 1,500 pupils. Located at 559 Cypress Avenue. Its reading scores place it in the top 70 percent of all public elementary schools in New York City.

INTERMEDIATE SCHOOL: IS 93, Ridgewood Intermediate School, grades 6-8, is located at 66-56 Forest Avenue. It has about 1,600 students. Its reading scores place it in the top 40 percent of all public middle schools in New York City.

HIGH SCHOOL: Grover Cleveland High School is located a short walk away at 2127 Himrod Street. It has about 2,800 students. Student achievement test scores are about average for a New York City High School. The school has a magnet Science/Math Institute and a magnet Business Program that are only open to Queens residents. Approximately 15 percent of the applicants for the Science/Math Institute are accepted.

Recreation

Forest Park: This 538-acre gem is a little more than 10 minutes away by car. For more information on this park see PARKS in the Where To Play In Queens section.

Local Park: Grover Cleveland Park covers 5.1 acres and is a five-minute walk away on Fairview Avenue.

(Also see Libraries, Private Schools, and Parochial Schools in the Appendix.)

St. John's University Area— Eighty-Second Road

(164th to 167th Street between 82nd Road and the Grand Central Parkway)

Four quiet blocks within walking distance of the affluent Jamaica Estates. Four blocks with almost no traffic. Four blocks of trees. Four blocks located between the 105-acre campus of St. John's University and the Art Deco buildings of the Queens Hospital Center (on its quiet side). Four blocks within three minutes of the crossroads of the Grand Central Parkway, the Van Wyck Expressway and the Jackie Robinson Parkway—all of which allow you to travel quickly in any direction. If this peace and convenience, plus handsome, solidly built, brick row houses, appeals to you, then 82nd Road between 164th and 167th Streets may be where you'd like to live. The cost would be considerably less than in many neighborhoods with fewer advantages.

There are several bus lines within a 10-minute walk. The F train station is on Hillside Avenue and Parsons Boulevard, about a mile away. It is served by two bus lines on Parsons Boulevard. Excellent access to parkways and expressways makes it only a matter of minutes to get to all of the exciting places to eat and shop in the borough, be it the upscale restaurants and movie theaters of Forest Hills or the stores and Asian restaurants of downtown Flushing. If Manhattan is your destination, the roadways make for quick, easy travel and you are assured of a parking space when you return home.

Two large parks are within 10 minutes, by car. To the east is the 350-acre Cunningham Park, with its tennis center and ballfields; to the west is the 538-acre Forest Park, with its 18-hole golf course, bandshell for outdoor concerts, horseback riding trails, carousel, tennis courts, and field activities.

Higher educational institutions are also easily accessed. St. John's University, a moderately priced private institution, is a few hundred feet away. Queens College, the star of the CUNY system, is about 10 minutes away by car and offers a quality education at minimum cost.

Real Estate

The market value of these substantial, brick, two-story homes ranges from $200,000 to $225,000.

Transportation

HIGHWAYS: Access to the nearby Grand Central Parkway takes less than five minutes. Thanks to the superb interconnected highway system in Queens, you can be in Manhattan in about 25 minutes, or in Nassau County in only 15 minutes. Both LaGuardia and Kennedy airports are only 15 minutes away. And almost any part of Queens can be reached in less than 30 minutes.

SUBWAYS: It takes about 10 minutes to walk to the E and F trains at the 169th Street-Hillside Avenue station. From there, it's 29 minutes to Lexington Avenue-53rd Street, 35 minutes to Rockefeller Center, 42 minutes to Grand Central-42nd Street, and 46 minutes to 23rd Street-6th Avenue.

EXPRESS BUSES: The QM1 and QM1A stop on Union Turnpike at 164th Street, about a 10-minute walk away. Both buses will get you to 3rd Avenue and 57th Street in Manhattan in about 50 minutes. An added attraction is the fact that both buses are in service on weekends.

Shopping

Within walking distance (on Union Turnpike) are a number of small service stores that include a beauty parlor, a candy/newspaper store, a dry cleaners, a delicatessen, a nail salon, a pharmacy, as well as a laundromat and pizza parlors. A Burger King, Dunkin Donuts, Seven/Eleven, and a Chinese take-out are also within walking distance. Better yet, also nearby on Union Turnpike, is a superior diner (the Hilltop) and three restaurants (two Chinese and one Italian). Further east on Union Turnpike, beginning about a mile away, are a large number of additional stores and more restaurants.

Education

ELEMENTARY SCHOOL: PS 131, grades K-6, about 800 pupils. Located at 84th Avenue and 172nd Street. Its reading scores place it in the top 20 percent of all public elementary schools in New York City.

JUNIOR HIGH SCHOOL: JHS 216, G.J. Ryan Junior High School, grades 7-9, is located at 64-20 175th Street. It has about 1,200 students. Its reading scores place it in the top 20 percent of all public middle schools in New York City.

HIGH SCHOOL: Jamaica High School is located at 167-01 Gothic Drive near the community of Jamaica Estates. Its approximately 2,500 students attend school in an architecturally imposing building built in 1927. Academically, the school's level of achievement compares favorably with the average level of achievement for all public high schools in New York City. In fact, at graduation nearly 90 percent of Jamaica students enroll in a college. The school has four magnet programs that are only open to Queens residents: Legal Studies Institute Program, Finance Institute Program, Computer Science Institute Program, and Computer in Business Program.

Recreation

Forest Park, Flushing Meadow Park, Cunningham Park, and Kissena Park are five to 10 minutes away by car. For more information see PARKS in the Where To Play In Queens section.

Local Park: About a five-minute walk away is the 4.0-acre Thomas Edison High School Playground on 164th Place.

(Also see Libraries, Private Schools, and Parochial Schools in the Appendix.)

Sunnyside

(Sunnyside Gardens area, 43rd to 49th Streets between Skillman to Barnett Avenues)

Sunnyside Gardens, in Sunnyside, offers its residents a discrete community environment of leafy tree-lined streets, moderately priced homes, and generous amounts of safe, private open space—ideal for children, gardeners, and loungers. Best of all, this urban idyll is situated only minutes from the 59th Street Bridge, which connects Queens to midtown Manhattan.

Sunnyside Gardens is a community within a community. Developed as a utopian experiment in community living in the mid to late 1920's, Sunnyside Gardens is a 77-acre enclave within the larger Sunnyside neighborhood. The enclave consists of: 600 two-story row houses, divided into one-, two-, and three-family units; several apartment buildings, including a cooperative; two community parks; and neighborhood stores. In the 1930's, the Phipps Houses garden apartments, 51-01 39th Avenue, were built on two blocks adjacent to the main development. The apartments surround a large landscaped interior court. The complex also has a day care center, meeting rooms, and rooftop terraces.

At first glance the streets in Sunnyside Gardens appear to be like most residential streets in the city—long rectangular blocks lined with houses with small gardens in front and back. But the appearance is deceiving, because behind the private backyards is a common open green that runs the length of each block, providing large interior garden spaces which are out of sight of the street and passerbys, but under the friendly watch of neighbors.

The pleasing arrangement of the housing, open space, and trees is enhanced by differences in the brickwork, doorways, roof shapes, and materials used in each group of houses. Yet, except for a walkway in midblock, the houses offer a solid facade that, while friendly, is self contained.

In the thriving Sunnyside neighborhood surrounding Sunnyside Gardens large numbers of neighborhood stores service the gamut of urban needs. Movie theatres, pubs, and modest restaurants are also nearby. The shopping area is a social gathering place for neighbors and is convenient and safe.

Transportation is also convenient. The 46th Street/Bliss Avenue station of the number 7 subway line is only 13 minutes from Grand Central Station. The Q60 bus runs along nearby Queens Boulevard and goes over the Queensboro Bridge to 60th Street in Manhattan. Most residents of Sunnyside Gardens with a car find a parking space on the local streets, although some garage space is also available.

Real Estate

Based on recent sales, the market value of one-family houses on these lovely tree-lined streets starts at about $225,000. Prices increase up to the low $300,000s for two- and three-family houses.

Transportation

HIGHWAYS: It is quick and easy to get to Manhattan from Sunnyside. A short ride on Queens Boulevard and over the 59th Street/Queensboro Bridge can bring you to Bloomingdale's in 10 minutes. The Queens Midtown Tunnel provides an almost equally fast, alternate route that takes you to 36th Street in Manhattan in as little as 15 minutes. LaGuardia Airport can be reached in little more than 10 minutes via the Brooklyn-Queens Expressway and Grand Central Parkway. Almost any part of Queens can be reached within a half hour, thanks to the modern, interconnected, network of parkways and expressways in the borough.

SUBWAYS: From the 46th Street-Bliss Street station of the number 7 train you can reach Grand Central-42nd Street in only 13 minutes, 42nd Street-Times Square in 16 minutes, 14th Street-Union Square in 21 minutes, and 34th Street-Herald Square in 29 minutes.

BUSES: The Q60 takes you to 60th Street in Manhattan via the Queensboro Bridge.

Shopping

There are four nearby shopping streets: Skillman Avenue and 43rd Avenue are the two closest and have mainly convenience stores. Queens Boulevard, between 42nd and 48th Street has stores that serve both the local area and the wider community. Greenpoint Avenue, which cuts into Queens Boulevard at a diagonal, has additional stores.

Sunnyside has many restaurants with a wide range of cuisines, including Romanian, Korean, Japanese, Indian, Hispanic, Chinese, Greek, Irish, and health food. There are also several international food stores.

Sunnyside has stores to meet most every need. There are banks, beauty parlors, barber shops, dry cleaners, groceries, fruit-and-vegetable stores, laundromats, meat markets, pharmacies, pizza parlors, travel agents, and video stores. Other stores include a bagel shop, bakery, coffee house, gourmet deli, and a supermarket.

Education

ELEMENTARY SCHOOL: PS 150, grades K-6, about 1,100 pupils. Located at 40-01 43rd Avenue. Its reading scores place it in the top 15 percent of all public elementary schools in New York City.

INTERMEDIATE SCHOOL: IS 125, Woodside Intermediate School, grades 5-8, is located at 46-02 47th Avenue. It has about 1,700 students. Its reading scores place it in the top 40 percent of all public middle schools in New York City.

HIGH SCHOOL: William Cullen Bryant High School is located at 48-10 31st Avenue. It has about 4,300 students. Student achievement test scores are about average for a New York City High School. The school has a higher than average rate—30 percent—of students who are recent immigrants, mainly Hispanic and Chinese. The school offers a screened magnet Math-Science Enrichment Program that is only open to Queens residents.

Recreation

Forest Park: This 538-acre gem is about 15 minutes away by car. For more information on this park and its facilities see PARKS in the Where To Play In Queens section.

Torsney Playground: This 2-acre playground on 43rd Street and 3-acre Windmuller Park on 52nd Street are both less than a 10-minute walk away.

(Also see Libraries, Private Schools, and Parochial Schools in the Appendix.)

Appendix

Libraries

Addisleigh Park
The St. Albans Branch Library, at 191-05 Linden Boulevard, is less than a 15-minute walk away. Circulation of books and other materials has increased over the past few years and is now at about 96,000.

Astoria
The Steinway Branch Library, at 21-45 31st Street, is less than a five-minute walk away. Circulation of books and other materials has remained steady over the past several years, at about 260,000.

Auburndale
The East Flushing Branch Library, at 196-36 Northern Boulevard, is about a 10-minute walk away. Circulation of books and other materials has increased over the past several years and is now 205,000.

Bayside
The Bayside Branch Library is located at 214-20 Northern Boulevard, less than a five-minute drive away. Circulation of books and other materials is about 506,000.

Bowne Park
The McGoldrick Branch Library, at 155-06 Roosevelt Avenue, is a 10-minute walk away. Circulation of books and other materials is about 335,000.

Briarwood
The Briarwood Branch Library, at 85-12 Main Street, is about a 10-minute walk away. Circulation of books and other materials has grown steadily over the past few years and is about 218,000.

College Point
The Poppenhusen Branch Library, at 121-23 14th Avenue, is a two-minute walk away. Circulation of books and other materials totals about 137,000.

Douglaston

The Douglaston-Little Neck Branch Library is located at 249-01 Northern Boulevard, less than a 10-minute drive away. Circulation of books and other materials is about 175,000.

Flushing

The Mitchell-Linden Branch Library, located at 29-42 Union Street, is a five-minute walk away. Circulation of books and other materials has increased over the past few years to about 250,000.

Forest Hills Gardens & Vicinity
Forest Hills—The Closes

The Forest Hills Branch Library, at 108-19 71st Avenue, is less than a 15-minute walk away. Circulation of books and other materials has increased slightly over the past several years, to about 475,000. A second branch library, The North Forest Park Branch Library, is located in the southern part of Forest Hills at 98-27 Metropolitan Avenue. It has a circulation of 208,000 and is about a five-minute car ride away.

Forest Hills—North of Queens Boulevard

The Forest Hills Branch Library, at 108-19 71st Avenue, is about a 10-minute walk away. Circulation of books and other materials has increased slightly over the past several years, to about 475,000.

Hollis
Holliswood

The Hollis Branch Library, at 202-05 Hillside Avenue, is about a 10-minute walk away. Circulation of books and other materials is about 121,000. The Queens Central Library, at 89-11 Merrick Boulevard, is a five-minute car ride away. This is the main library of the Queens library system. It is a relatively new building with a superlative variety of resource material. A large public parking lot is adjacent to the facility, which also can be reached easily by subway or bus. Circulation of books and other materials has grown rapidly over the past several years and is now about 1,900,000.

Jackson Heights

The Jackson Heights Branch Library, at 33-51 81st Street, is within easy walking distance. Circulation of books and other materials has continued to increase over the past few years and now totals almost 600,000, among the highest circulation figures for a branch library in Queens.

Jamaica

The Queens Central Library, at 89-11 Merrick Boulevard, is a 15-minute walk or five-minute car ride away. This is the main library of the Queens library system. It is a relatively new building with a superlative variety of resource material. A large public parking lot is adjacent to the facility, which also can be reached easily by subway or bus. Circulation of books and other materials has grown rapidly over the past several years and is now about 1,900,000.

Jamaica Estates

The Hillcrest Branch Library, at 187-05 Union Turnpike, is a 10- to 15-minute walk away. Circulation of books and other materials has remained stable over the past several years, but with a circulation of about 400,000, this branch is still among the largest in the Queens Library system.

Kew Gardens

The Briarwood Branch Library, at 85-12 Main Street, is about a 10-minute walk away. Circulation of books and other materials has grown steadily over the past few years and is about 218,000

Kew Gardens—Park Lane South

The Richmond Hill Branch Library, at 118-14 Hillside Avenue, is less than a 10-minute walk away. Circulation of books and other materials has increased over the years to about 300,000.

Laurelton

The Laurelton Branch Library, at 134-26 225th Street, is a 10-to-15-minute walk away. Circulation of books and other materials has increased slightly over the past several years and is now about 107,000.

Long Island City

The Court Square Branch Library, at 25-01 Jackson Avenue, is a few minutes walk away. Circulation of books and other materials is about 122,000, more than triple the circulation of ten years ago. Employees in the CitiBank office building account for most of the increase.

Malba

The Whitestone Branch Library, at 151-10 14th Road, is about five minutes away by car. Circulation of books and other materials has grown steadily to about 254,000.

Richmond Hill—Condo
Richmond Hill North

The Richmond Hill Branch Library, at 118-14 Hillside Avenue, is about five minutes away by car. Circulation of books and other materials has increased over the years to about 300,000.

Ridgewood—Sixty-Ninth Avenue
Ridgewood—Stockholm Street
The Ridgewood Branch Library is located at 20-12 Madison Avenue, less than a 10-minute walk away from Sixty-Ninth Avenue and 15 minutes from Stockholm Street. Circulation of books and other materials is about 300,000.

St. John's University Area–Eighty-Second Road
The Hillcrest Branch Library, at 187-05 Union Turnpike, is a five-minute car ride away. Circulation of books and other materials has remained stable over the past several years, but with a circulation of about 400,000, this branch is still among the largest in the Queens Library system. The Queens Central Library, at 89-11 Merrick Boulevard, is a five-minute car ride away. This is the main library of the Queens library system. It is a relatively new building with a superlative variety of resource material. A large public parking lot is adjacent to the facility, which also can be reached easily by subway or bus. Circulation of books and other materials has grown rapidly over the past several years and is now about 1,900,000.

Sunnyside
There are two libraries to choose from, each about a 10-minute walk away. They are the recently renovated Woodside Branch Library at 54-22 Skillman Avenue and the Sunnyside Branch Library at 43-06 Greenpoint Avenue. Their combined circulation of books and other materials is 575,000, with slightly more than one-half of the circulation attributable to the Sunnyside branch.

Private Schools

Eleven private schools serve Queens. Six schools provide an elementary school education, two provide middle and high school classes, and three provide classes from elementary through high school. The school's name, address, zip code, telephone number, number of students enrolled, cost of yearly tuition, and grade levels taught is listed below. There are also many parochial schools in Queens. For a list of parochial schools that serve the Queens neighborhoods mentioned in this book, see the Appendix, page 178.

Christopher Robin Elementary and High School, 222-16 Merrick Road, Springfield Gardens, New York 11413: (718) 525-1330. The school enrolls about 160 students in grades 1 to 12. Tuition is about $4,400, slightly less for the lower grades. Close to 100 percent of the students go on to college.

Garden School, 33-16 79th Street, Jackson Heights, New York 11372: (718) 335-6363. The school accepts students from nursery school (age two) through grade 12. Total enrollment is about 375. The school has an after-school program until 6:00 p.m. Tuition ranges from about $7,200 for the lower school to $7,800 for the upper school. Nearly 100 percent of the graduates go on to college.

Highland Elementary/Middle School, 193-10 Peck Avenue, Fresh Meadows, New York 11365: (718) 357-4747. The school enrolls about 150 students in grades K-8. Tuition ranges from $5,400 to $6,600. There is an early drop-off and an after-school program. The school helps to prepare students for acceptance to the city's specialized high schools, such as the Bronx High School of Science and Stuyvesant High School.

Ideal Montessori School, 87-41 165th Street, Jamaica, New York 11432: (718) 523-6237. The school enrolls 160 pupils in grades preK-8 (ages 3 to 14). Tuition is $3,500.

Kew Forest School, 119-17 Union Turnpike, Forest Hills, New York 11375: (718) 268-4667. The school has 100 students enrolled in grades 1-5 and 280 in grades 6-12. Tuition, including lunches and books, ranges from $8,400 for the 1st grade to $9,500 for grade 12. All of their graduates go on to college.

Montessori School of Forest Hills, 67-04 Austin Street, Forest Hills, New York 11375: (718) 275-0173. The school has 140 pupils in grades K-6. Tuition is $5,600 for grades 1-6; kindergarten is slightly less. There is also a half-day preK program. French and music instruction is provided from nursery school through the 6th grade.

Montessori School of New York International, 55-30 Junction Boulevard, Corona, New York 11368: (718) 857-3341. The school serves approximately 70 children from, preK-grade 8. Tuition ranges from $5,500 for a full-day kindergarten to $7,000 for grade 8. There are extended hours, as well as a nursery program starting at age two and one-half.

North Side School (Montessori), 263-10 Union Turnpike, Floral Park, New York 11004: (718) 343-5050. The school enrolls approximately 100 pupils in grades preK-6. Tuition for grades 1-6 is $5,950, including books. There are twice weekly French, music, and physical education lessons for all students. There is also a half-day nursery program for children as young as two and one-half.

Whitestone Academy, 150-34 12th Avenue, Whitestone, New York 11357: (718) 767-0773. The school serves about 100 students in grades 7-12. Tuition ranges from $4,800 to $5,800. Nearly all of their graduates go on to college.

Windsor School, 136-23 Sanford Avenue, Flushing, New York 11355: (718) 359-8300. The school serves about 150 students in grades 6-12. Tuition ranges from $10,400 to $12,500. Nearly 100 percent of their graduates go on to college. In addition to American students, the school attracts foreign students.

United Nations International School, 173-53 Croydon Road, Jamaica, New York 11432: (718) 658-6166. The school serves 225 students in grades K-8. Tuition ranges from $12,000 to $12,700. New facilities at the school include a library/media center, a gym, and a science lab. The school prepares students for an International Baccalaureate Diploma. After grade 8, most students transfer to the school's Manhattan campus.

Parochial Schools

Listed below are parochial schools within a reasonable distance of each of the areas featured in this book. This is not a complete listing of all parochial schools in Queens—for those willing to travel farther there are additional schools available. See also the listing, PRIVATE SCHOOLS, in the Appendix. Note that some parochial schools are listed more than once since they are convenient to more than one area. All telephone numbers shown are in area code (718) in Queens.

ADDISLEIGH PARK

PreK-8

Allen Christian School	111-54 Merrick Boulevard	657-1676
St. Catherine of Siena School	118-22 Riverton Street	528-1857

High School

Dominican Commercial High	161-02 89th Avenue	739-2060

ASTORIA

PreK-8

Immaculate Conception School	21-47 29th Street	728-1969
Our Lady of Mt. Carmel School	23-15 Newtown Avenue	728-8376
St. Francis of Assisi School	21-18 46th Street	726-9405

High School

St. John's Prep School	21-21 Crescent Street	721-7200

K-12 School

St. Demetrios Greek American	30-03 30th Drive	728-1754

AUBURNDALE

PreK-8

Bayside Lutheran School	164-05 35th Avenue	961-6062
Flushing Christian School	158-15 Oak Avenue	445-3533
Lutheran Schl Flushing & Bayside	44-10 192nd Street	225-5502
Our Lady of Blessed Sacrament	202-00 35th Avenue	229-4434
St. Andrew Avellino School	38-50 158th Street	359-7887

St. Kevin School	45-50 195th Street	357-8110
St. Mary's Nativity School	146-00 Jasmine Avenue	359-1800
St. Robert Bellarmine School	56-10 214th Street	225-3181
William Spyropoulos School	196-10 Northern Boulevard	357-5583
Yeshiva Institute	43-00 171st Street	762-7070

High School

Holy Cross High School	26-20 Francis Lewis Blvd.	886-7250

BAYSIDE

PreK-8

Sacred Heart School	216-33 38th Avenue	631-4804
St. Anastasia School	41-05 245th Street	631-3153

(See the listing of parochial schools in Auburndale for the addresses and telephone numbers of schools that also serve Bayside: Bayside Lutheran School; Lutheran School of Flushing & Bayside; Our Lady of the Blessed Sacrament School; St. Kevin School; St. Robert Bellarmine School; William Spyropoulos School; Yeshiva Institute; and Holy Cross High School.)

BOWNE PARK

PreK-8

Bayside Lutheran School	164-05 35th Avenue	961-6062
St. Andrew Avellino School	35-50 158th Street	359-7887
St. Mel's School	154-24 26th Avenue	539-8211
Yeshiva Institute	43-00 171st Street	762-7070

High School

Holy Cross High School	26-20 Francis Lewis Boulevard	886-7250

BRIARWOOD

PreK-8

Holy Family School	74-15 175th Street	591-6438
Immaculate Conception School	179-14 Dalny Road	739-5933
Jamaica Day School St. Demetrios	84-35 152nd Street	526-2622
Our Lady Queen of Martyrs School	72-55 Austin Street	263-2622
St. Nicholas of Tolentine School	80-22 Parsons Boulevard	380-1900

High School

Archbishop Malloy High School	83-53 Manton Street	441-2100
Ezra Academy	119-45 Union Turnpike	268-4667
Mary Lewis Academy	176-21 Wexford Terrace	297-2120
St. Francis Prep High School	61-00 Francis Lewis Boulevard	423-8810
Shevach High School	75-09 Main Street	263-0525
Yeshiva University H.S. for Girls	86-86 Palo Alto Street	479-8550

COLLEGE POINT

PreK-8

Holy Trinty School	14-51 143rd Street	746-1479
St. Fidelis School	124-06 14th Avenue	539-2628
St. John Lutheran School	123-07 22nd Avenue	463-4790
St. Paul's Episcopal School	13-21 College Point Boulevard	762-4100

High School

St. Agnes Academic High School	13-20 124th Street	353-6276

DOUGLASTON

PreK-8

Sacred Heart School	216-33 38th Avenue	631-4804
St. Anastasia School	45-05 245th Stree	631-3153
St. Robert Bellarmine School	56-10 214th Street	225-3181

High School

St. Francis Prep High School	61-00 Francis Lewis Boulevard	423-8810

FLUSHING

PreK-8

Bayside Lutheran School	164-05 35th Avenue	961-6062
Holy Trinity School	14-51 143rd Street	746-1479
Immanuel Lutheran School	12-10 150th Street	767-5656
St. Mary's Nativity School	146-00 Jasmine Avenue	359-1800
St. Andrew Avellino School	35-50 158th Street	359-7887
St. Luke's School	16-01 150th Place	746-3833
St. Mel's School	154-24 26th Avenue	539-8211
St. Michael School	136-58 41st Avenue	961-0246

High School

Holy Cross High School	26-20 Francis Lewis Boulevard	886-7250

FOREST HILLS GARDENS & VICINITY
FOREST HILLS —NORTH OF QUEENS BOULEVARD
FOREST HILLS—THE CLOSES

PreK-8

Our Lady of Mercy School	70-25 Kessel Street	793-2086
Our Lady Queen of Martyrs School	72-55 Austin Street	263-2622
Our Saviour Lutheran School	64-33 Woodhaven Boulevard	897-4343
Yeshiva Ohr Yisroel	66-20 Thornton Place	263-6242

High School

Ezra Academy	119-45 Union Turnpike	263-5500
Shevach High School	75-09 Main Street	263-0525
Archbishop Molloy High School	83-53 Manton Street	441-2100

HOLLIS, HOLLISWOOD, JAMAICA ESTATES

PreK-8

Holy Family School	74-15 175th Street	591-6438
Holy Trinity Community School	90-20 191st Street	465-0521
Immaculate Conception School	179-14 Dalny Road	739-5933
Jamaica Day School St. Demetrios	84-35 152nd Street	526-2622
St. Nicholas of Tolentine School	80-22 Parsons Boulevard	380-1900

High School

Archbishop Molloy High School	83-53 Manton Street	441-2100
Mary Lewis Academy	176-21 Wexford Terrace	297-2120
St. Francis Prep High School	61-00 Francis Lewis Boulevard	423-8810
Yeshiva University H.S. for Girls	86-86 Palo Alto Street	479-8550

JACKSON HEIGHTS

PreK-8

Blessed Sacrament School	34-43 93rd Street	446-4449
Our Lady of Fatima School	25-38 80th Street	429-7031
St. Joan of Arc School	35-27 82nd Street	639-9020

High School

Monsignor McClancy High School 71-06 31st Avenue   898-3800

JAMAICA

PreK-8

Al-Iman Elementary & Jr. H.S.	89-89 Van Wyck Expressway	297-6520
Presentation Blessed Virgin Mary	88-13 Parsons Boulevard	739-2003
St. Peter Claver School	149-18 Jamaica Avenue	739-3221

High School

Dominican Commercial H.S.	161-02 89th Avenue	739-2060
Mary Lewis Academy	176-21 Wexford Terrace	297-2120
Yeshiva University H.S. for Girls	86-86 Palo Alto Street	479-8550

KEW GARDENS AND PARK LANE SOUTH

PreK-8

Benedict Joseph Labre School	94-25 117th Street	unlisted
Holy Child Jesus School	111-02 86th Avenue	849-3988
Bais Yakov Academy for Girls	124-50 Metropolitan Avenue	847-5352
Our Lady of the Cenacle School	87-25 136th Street	657-6690
Our Lady Queen of Martyrs School	72-55 Austin Street	263-2622
Yeshiva Tifereth Moshe	83-06 Abingdon Road	846-7300
Yeshivat Ohr Haiim	86-06 135th Street	658-7066

High School

Ezra Academy	119-45 Union Turnpike	263-5500
Shaar Hatorah High School	117-06 84th Avenue	unlisted
Shevach High School	75-09 Main Street	263-0525
Archbishop Molloy High School	83-53 Manton Street	441-2100

LAURELTON

PreK-8

Cambria Center Gifted Children	233-10 Linden Boulevard	341-1991
Christ Lutheran School	248-03 Francis Lewis Boulevard	525-6884
Linden 7th Day Adventist School	137-01 228th Street	527-6868
Sacred Heart School	115-50 221st Street	527-0123

St. Clare School	137-25 Brookville Boulevard	528-3191
St. Joseph's Parish Day School	99-10 217th Lane	464-8913
St. Pius X School	147-65 249th Street	525-7858

High School

Bethel Christian Learning Center	219-09 Linden Boulevard	unlisted

LONG ISLAND CITY

PreK-8

Evangel Christian School	39-21 Crescent Street	937-9600
St. Rita School	36-12 12th Street	729-1594

High School

St. John's Prep School	21-21 Crescent Street	721-7200
Greater New York Academy	41-32-58th Street	639-1752

MALBA

PreK-8

Holy Trinity School	14-51 143rd Street	746-1479
Immanuel Lutheran School	12-10 150th Street	767-5656
St. Fidelis School	124-06 14th Avenue	539-2628
St. John Lutheran School	123-07 22nd Avenue	463-4790
St. Luke's School	16-01 150th Place	746-3833
St. Paul's Episcopal School	13-21 College Point Boulevard	762-4100

High School

St. Agnes Academic High School	13-20 124th Street	353-6276

RICHMOND HILL CONDO
RICHMOND HILL NORTH

PreK-8

Bais Yakov Academy for Girls	124-50 Metropolitan Avenue	847-5352
Benedict Joseph Labre School	94-25 117th Street	unlisted
Holy Child Jesus School	111-02 86th Avenue	849-3988
Nativity of Blessed Virgin Mary	101-50 92nd Street	845-3691
St. Elizabeth School	94-01 85th Street	641-6900

St. Mary Gate of Heaven School	101-20 105th Avenue	846-0689
St. Stanislaus Bishop & Martyr	90-01 101st Avenue	835-9447
St. Thomas Apostle School	87-40 88th Street	847-3904
Yeshiva Tifrereth Moshe	83-06 Abingdon Road	846-7300

High School

Archbishop Molloy High School	83-53 Manton Street	441-210
Shaar Hatorah High School	117-06 84th Avenue	unlisted

RIDGEWOOD—SIXTY-NINTH AVENUE AND STOCKHOLM STREET

PreK-8

Our Lady of the Miraculous Medal	62-01 61st Street	821-2221
St. Aloysius School	360 Seneca Avenue	821-7384
St. Matthias School	58-15 Catalpa Avenue	381-7304
St. Pancras School	68-20 Myrtle Avenue	821-6721

High School

Christ the King High School	68-02 Metropolitan Avenue	366-7400

ST. JOHN'S UNIVERSITY AREA—EIGHTY-SECOND ROAD
(See Briarwood parochial schools; they are convenient to Eighty-Second Road.)

SUNNYSIDE

PreK-8

Queen Of Angels School	41-12 44th Street	786-2990
Razi School	55-11 Queens Boulevard	779-0711
St. Raphael School	48-29 37th Street	784-0482
St. Sebastian School	39-76 58th Street	429-1982
St. Teresa School	50-15 44th Street	784-0178

High School

Greater New York Academy	41-32 58th Street	639-1752
Monsignor McClancy High School	71-06 31st Avenue	898-3800